I Am My Father's Child

A True Story of Mystery, History, Betrayal, and Forgiveness

Kim Cook

Disclaimer:

This book is a work of nonfiction, drawn from the author's memories, reflections, and presentations of real events throughout the period of her life described in these pages. Every effort has been made to recount experiences faithfully. Names, locations, and identifying details reman unchanged. Dialogue and scenes are reconstructed from memory and reflect the author's best attempts to recall them accurately.

I Am My Father's Child

DEDICATION

This book is dedicated to my children. I hope it will show you what you come from. Take the strength, courage, and compassion from your ancestors. Leave behind the drama and hurt, and most of all learn to forgive. Life will present you with many ups and downs. It's what you choose to do with them that matters. Find your strength in God.

This book is also dedicated to the many friends who have become family: all the people who have passed through my life, each becoming a tile in the mosaic of my life. And finally to Mark McNease, who's taken all my words and helped turn it into a story to share.

And to my extraordinary friend Brenda, who took the time to read each word and encourage me on this journey to the finish.

So many people have encouraged me to write the story of true love, deceit, hurt, and forgiveness. I have been blessed to come out on the other side of all these things with a life that is completely full of adventures, warm family, and amazing friends. It took me a lifetime to live the story, and now it's your turn to read it.

I Am My Father's Child

INTRODUCTION

In every life, there are moments that shimmer just beneath the surface of memory—encounters, decisions, and turning points that, at the time, felt ordinary but would come to shape the very fabric of who we are. This book is a journey into such moments: the recollections of a daughter navigating the joys and sorrows of family, the unpredictability of change, and the search for belonging across places and decades. Woven through these pages are the voices of those I have loved and learned from, especially my father, whose gentle wisdom guided me through the tumult and beauty of growing up. As I open these doors to my past, I invite you to step inside, to witness the laughter and grief, the certainty and doubt, and perhaps find echoes of your own story along the way.

- Kim Cook (aka Sunshine)

I Am My Father's Child

CHAPTER ONE

An Orchid Corsage

1973

The night my father called himself my date, I wore a green dress that matched my eyes and a white orchid corsage that smelled faintly of salt and sweetness. I didn't know it then, but he was teaching me what love should look like.

It was 1973, and I was a young, naïve girl of sixteen. The Queen Mary still felt new in her harbor home in Long Beach, California. The old ocean liner rested proudly at the dock, grand and graceful, her decks echoing with stories of another time. That night, one of those stories became my own.

My father, George Hlopak, had promised me a special evening, though he kept the details quiet. He picked me up from school that afternoon, his hair neat, his shirt crisp, and a spark of mischief in his voice. "We have a few errands to run," he said, and I could tell by his tone that it was no ordinary day.

We stopped at a dress shop, the kind with chandeliers and saleswomen who still called customers "Dear." He sat on a velvet settee while I tried on two dresses, waiting patiently as I stepped out from the fitting room each time. When I appeared in the green one, he smiled in that quiet, certain way of his. "That one," he said. "It matches your beautiful green eyes." And that was that. The green dress became mine.

Later that evening at home, when I came out of my room ready for dinner, he was waiting with a clear box in his hands. Inside was a white orchid corsage, the kind worn at proms and formal dances. He took it out carefully and fastened it around my wrist.

"Tonight I'm not your dad," he said, his voice gentle but sure. "I'm your date."

He was teaching me something that night without ever saying it directly. He was showing me how a girl should expect to be treated, what respect and care looked like, what it meant to be valued. I didn't have the words for it yet, but I understood the feeling.

When we arrived at the Queen Mary, he opened the car door for me and offered his arm. The ship rose above us like a palace on the water, her decks glowing beneath the California sky. He had served in the Navy, and I think part of him always belonged to the sea. He seemed completely at home as we walked up the gangway, the lights from the harbor dancing in his eyes.

An ocean liner is not a cruise ship. Ocean liners are smaller than their more familiar cousins, and designed to carry passengers between continents. They are *not* designed to be stationery floating hotels, restaurants and tourist attractions, but that's exactly what happened to the RMS Queen Mary when, in 1967 after a long and distinguished career that included serving in World War II as a troop carrier, she sailed to Long Beach, California, where she remains to this day.

Her maiden voyage began on May 27, 1936, when the ship departed from Southampton, England. Spectacular at the time, the Queen Mary featured five dining areas and lounges, two cocktail bars and swimming pools, a grand ballroom, and a squash court. There was even a small hospital. Considered the only civilized way to travel by the rich and famous of its day, the grand ship captured hearts and imaginations on both sides of the Atlantic.

The Queen Mary began her life as one of the Cunard line's two "Queens," the other being the RMS Queen Elizabeth, serving together as a weekly express between Southampton and New York. After a distinguished tour carrying over 800,000 military personnel in the battle against European fascism known as World War II, she returned to passenger service. As a reward for its years of civilian and military service, the ship was given a permanent home on the Southern California coast. Countless people have enjoyed her presence ever since, many with no idea of her illustrious history.

I was one of those people, and in 1973 I had the pleasure of an evening on the Queen Mary that imbedded itself into my memory in the way only life-determining events can. Not so much life-*altering* — that would come later, more than once — but in ways that determined who I became as an adult, a woman who had still been a girl then unaware of the challenges we're required to face and overcome in the course of a lifetime. That night my life was still magical, and the gentle, funny, smart, kind magician at the center of it was my father.

George Hlopak, Jr. was a police officer with the Plainfield, New Jersey, Police Department. Two years from retiring after putting in his required twenty, my father had assured us he would one day build a house in Malibu and we would live there, leaving New Jersey behind for a golden future in the Golden State. He'd sent my mother and me to live with his business partner Gene in Long Beach to get us away from a reality that had rocked Plainfield several years

3

earlier, its aftershocks still reverberating, and that had left him with a permanent back injury: the Plainfield riots of 1967. One of 59 riots that swept cities in the United States during what came to be called "The Long Hot Summer of 1967," the Plainfield riots were racially charged, violent upheavals that mirrored riots in Newark, just 18 miles away. It was a time of intense social disruption, and it came to Plainfield like a bomb dropped into a crowded market. One police officer, John Gleason, lost his life after a confrontation between rioters and a white motorcycle gang called the Pagans. My father did the job he was expected and proud to do, and managed to come through it alive but injured. A car hit him during the rioting, throwing him over the hood, and the resulting pain was both ever-present and a message from the future. His trips to the chiropractor became part of his life's routine, and ours. But that night, far away from the flashpoint of 1967 Plainfield, all that mattered was our evening together, what he wanted to teach me, and what I have never forgotten.

***

My father always wore dress slacks after his stint in the U.S. Navy, when he wasn't in his police uniform. Blue jeans were a foreign choice to him, something for less well-groomed men. He was always at his best, or tried to be, and how he appeared to himself and the world was important to him. Had he not met my mother while he was in the military, he would have stayed there and certainly achieved high rank, along with a military retirement. Life had other plans, however, and it took him to the Plainfield Police Department instead. Everything else seems unavoidable in hindsight, but isn't that true of every life? We don't always know where the journey is taking us until we've arrived, yet the path behind us looks as if it could have led us nowhere else.

All I knew of this particular evening was that we were going out to dinner, and that there was something special about it. Like most families, the three of us had eaten out

4

many times, but tonight it was to be just me and my father. There was something electric about it from the beginning.

Not only had my father taken it upon himself to treat me to a father-daughter date, but it was my first date by design. I was not worldly by any stretch of the imagination. I'd not had any date with a boy prior to that, and the central motive for the night was to show me what he considered the proper treatment of a girl, a soon-to-be-woman, by someone of the opposite sex. There were things my father wanted me to know about what was acceptable and what was not. He believed I should never accept anything beneath my own standards, which he was helping inform with this evening. I sensed that the way he was treating me was the way he wanted me to insist I be treated in the future, when the date was not my father.

***

My father's nickname was Sonny, which often matched his disposition and was the name everyone used for him. He was a man of firm beliefs and morals, as well as a man of kindness and compassion. He actually received thank you letters on occasion from someone he'd arrested or their loved ones, not for getting another criminal off the streets, but for helping set them on a better path.

"It's not about the crime," he once told me. "It's about the soul. If you can fix the soul, they won't commit the crime."

He also told me more than once that, "You are my sunshine, and don't let anyone ever put that out."

He was Sonny. I was his sunshine. That's what I knew when we got to the Queen Mary, and what I've always cherished.

After holding the car door for me the way he always did for my mother, we walked up the gangplank onto the ship. It had only been in its permanent home for six years, and it still felt like a new adventure.

It was here, once we'd been shown to our table and he'd held my chair out for me as he believed a gentleman ought to, he took my hand and held it in a way he hadn't before. "This is as far as a man should ever touch you until he marries you," he said. I knew he was showing me something with the entire experience, and that was part of it. He also told me that sex is in the mind and heart, starting in one and finding its way to the other.

These were "real life" lessons, intended for a daughter who was in many ways a babe-in-the-woods, and he knew it. He was cautioning me as well as preparing me. One of the things he said was also among the most unexpected: that once a woman finds the right man to marry, she can be as independent as she wants to be in public, but she must meet his needs in private. He believed marriage was a union of love, not just sex. Each person had a role to play in the relationship, and that was expected to be one of mine.

I don't recall dancing that night, but if they had a dance floor I'm sure we did. He'd taken us to the Rainbow Room once on a visit to New York City, and I'd danced with him there. The Rainbow Room remains an iconic and historic venue renowned for its stunning panoramic views of Manhattan. Originally opened in 1934, it has served as a symbol of elegance and sophistication, hosting high-profile events and celebrations over the decades. My father never worried about the cost, and when we danced it was always with my shoes on top of his as he led us in a turn around the room.

I think of that image sometimes, dancing with my father. In my mind's eye it can be anywhere … New York, Plainfield, Long Beach. He is still attempting to teach me as well as protect me from a world full of sharp edges, hard lessons, and a betrayal or two.

My father was an entrepreneur at heart. After his stint in the navy, he realized he needed a reliable pension, which led to him join the Plainfield Police Force. At the same time, his desire for business opportunities never left him.

He had business to attend to on that trip to California — a Carvel ice cream franchise to secure, some real estate in the desert where he owned a 350-unit trailer complex. He had other dealings I wasn't aware of at the time, especially given my age. My mother and father and I, along with his business partner Gene, would sometimes go to meetings together where I would wait outside while they made their deals.

Two days later my father flew back to Plainfield. He had taken me on a first date and done what he could to prepare me for at least some of the things to come. But there were other, darker, things neither of us could have anticipated. I consider that a blessing. It gave me memories of a place and time before the storm clouds gathered and the lightening struck.

Girls deserve to dance on the shoes of their fathers.

I was one of the lucky ones.

CHAPTER TWO

Paradise Lost

1941

World War II was a turning point in history, lasting from 1939 – 1945. The United States joined the war in September, 1941, after the devastating attack our our fleet at Pearl Harbor by the Japanese navy.

The *USS Shangri-La*, named after the mythical paradise of the same name, was among the aircraft carriers stationed in the Pacific during the conflict. For thousands of servicemen and sailors in that epic struggle, the paradise they found was in an afterlife, as casualties of the bloodiest and costliest war in human history. For others, the ships took them to Pacific islands that were anything but paradise. War and its attendant hardships did not lend themselves to that ideal.

George (nicknamed Sonny) Hlopak was a man of cultivated moral character who could also be naïve. He heard the call to service on December 7, 1941, when Japan attempted to obliterate the United States' naval fleet at Pearl Harbor. It was the ultimate red line, and the Japanese had crossed it with shocking fury and a swarm of kamikaze pilots flying Mitsubishi Zeros to their deaths. The tragedy for America was how many sailors they took with them in an act of aggression guaranteed to draw us into the global conflict consuming most of the Western world. Within days Germany and Italy declared war on the United States, and the nation launched itself into a fight for its survival. Sonny knew with the news of the attack in Hawaii, which would not become a state until 1959, that he had to do his part. There was only one problem: he was under the minimum age to enlist on his own, so he forged my grandmother's signature. It wasn't all that uncommon then for young men eager for service to sign a parent's signature on a military application. Some did it heeding a call to arms, others did it for adventure, and still others to get away from home. For my father, it was the right thing to do at the right time. His country needed him, and Sonny was not about to look the other way.

My paternal grandfather was another story, and a ghost in our lives. I never met him. My father would spend much of his life looking for his father, although he kept it a secret longing. As fate had it, the way it often does with the lives of mortals, George Hlopak, Sr. left his wife and two children the day his son went into the service, never to be seen again. Compounding that loss, father and son had made plans to get together that afternoon, but the Navy had other ideas. When they told you to ship out, that's what you did. There was no rescheduling, no putting it off until a more convenient time. Their meeting never happened ... and never would. My grandfather went off into mystery, and my father sailed away to fight the Land of the Rising Sun. The closest they ever came to seeing each other again was years later, when we were in a

9

San Francisco department store. An announcement came over the loudspeaker for a George Hlopak to please come to the customer service area. It's not a common surname, and my father hurried toward the entrance, just in time to see a man he believed was his father leaving through the front doors. He had disappeared a second time, and there wouldn't be another.

***

It's called "Crossing the Line" when a ship crosses the equator, with its own traditions being observed by sailors for centuries. It seems routine enough to the land-locked and those uninitiated into the ways of the seafarer, but it remains a cherished ritual in the navy. Even cruise ships on repositioning tours offer some version of it today, as if crossing a line in the ocean takes you from one world into another.

When ships were wooden, the ceremonies were meant to challenge young sailors on their first voyage out on the open sea. The men who'd never crossed the equator before were called "pollywogs," and were put through initiation rites that amounted to hazing on the high seas. Today those rituals are meant more to entertain the crew, with nothing too dangerous demanded of the men. Originally, the pollywogs were then inducted into the "Solemn Mysteries of the Ancient Order of the Deep," meaning that King Neptune had accepted them into his fold. A certificate was often awarded to each participating sailor as a rite of passage. My father told us he was given one because he'd crossed the equator twice. He eventually ended up on an island that he didn't want to be on, where he welcomed any way off.

***

"Good duty – a great crew and a great ship." Those are the words inscribed by my father on the back of a photograph of the *Sangri-la*. He was on that vessel, and he'd found himself

10

assigned to an island he would likely describe as more hell than heaven. He wanted off in any way he could accomplish it that did not include desertion.

As was often the case with my father, he eventually got what he wanted, in a most unexpected way. Wishes really do come true, if the right circumstances present themselves for wish fulfillment. Sonny was once again called to duty, but this time it was to help a friend in need, and help himself in the process.

My father had been platonic friends with a woman for several years. I found a photo of him years later with his arm around a woman, and when I asked my mother who she was, she said, "That was his first wife." She was as matter-of-fact about it as I was surprised.

Physical intimacy had not entered into his friendship with this mystery woman, whom I will call Mary. When he received a letter from her telling him she was pregnant, he knew it was not his child, and he knew what to do.

As hard as it is to imagine today, if a sailor was found to have a pregnant girlfriend back in the states he was sent home to get married and make a respectable woman out of her — not to mention making an honorable man of himself and a legitimate child of their offspring. For Mary, it was a chance to have her baby born with married parents, and for him it was a ticket off the island.

In a series of head-spinning events, he married his friend Mary, provided the child with a father, and almost immediately encountered the love of his life strolling down a sidewalk while he was still on leave. One day he was on one side of a street, and a woman he'd never seen before was on the other.

Her name was Loretta, but he didn't know that yet.

She was a stranger, but wouldn't be for long.

She was so startingly beautiful that my father Sonny, completely out of character for a normally shy and reserved man, put two of his fingers together, raised them to his lips, and *whistled*. It was the kind of two-fingered whistle you've

I Am My Father's Child

seen in movies and on TV, a bold, *listen up* whistle that can't be missed or ignored.

She heard the whistle and turned toward him.

"Hello, good lookin,' what you got cookin'?" he said, as he crossed the street where she was waiting to find out who this daring young man was.

Weeks later, they were married. Keep in mind my father was not a bigamist, so it's likely his marriage to his friend was annulled or invalidated in some other quiet, legal way. His true aim was Loretta, and he wasn't a man to miss his target.

Sonny was in love and he wasn't going anywhere. He'd intended to enlist for a second tour of duty, but fate had something else in mind. Once he met my mother Loretta, having fallen as hard as one person can for another, all bets were off and every wager was a winning one ... or so it seemed.

On the subject of gambling: my father grew up in a strict Southern Baptist household, raised with his older sister Ruth by their mother Edith once his father had fled the scene. Edith Hlopak was a classy woman, a bit on the stocky side. She often wore beautiful dresses with lace on them, and never slacks. She kept a hanky that was twisted up and somehow managed to stay tucked in her sleeve. She never wore long-sleeved dresses, even in winter when it might seem appropriate. She always had a sweater-coat over her dresses, which were handmade. She was a marvelous cook, and she would set a gorgeous Sunday table with linen and fine China arranged around a lovely centerpiece she made herself. Nothing was cheap: if she owned it, it had to be top quality.

Edith was also a kind woman, and a Bible reader at church. She could sing like a canary, with a voice that stood out among the others. She read her Bible daily, and she lived by it. She was a good woman, but her beliefs were deep and her rules were rigid. There was no television in their home, which wasn't all that unusual at a time when televisions were just beginning their ascent to cultural dominance. There was also no radio, not board games, no playing cards, and the primary source of reading material was a bible. My father even told us once that when he first encountered playing cards in the Navy, he had no idea what to do with them.

My aunt Ruth, his sister, was what you might call back then an old maid, a term used for a woman who lived with her mother or parents and took care of them. She was at least as strict as Edith, but also very fun in some ways. She taught me how to bake, and we would work together in the kitchen. I would sneak a taste of the raw dough from the chocolate chip cookies we were making. She'd frown and tell me it was unhealthy. Aunt Ruth was tall and stocky like her mother. She never wore makeup or painted her fingernails, and she wore her brown hair in very tight curls. She took very good care of Grandma Edith and we had such wonderful Sunday dinners at their house.

Sonny was not a worldly man, as you might imagine growing up in such a strict household, despite making decisions later on that might seem worldly and impetuous. As strong a guiding hand as my father was, he went his own way when it suited him. He joined the Navy with a forged parental signature because he was under age at the time. He married his friend Mary to make sure she wouldn't be an outcast in a society that still took a harsh view of unmarried pregnant women. And now he married for love to Loretta, whose stride across a street had caught his eye and captured his heart.

Loretta was Polish Catholic, a woman of whom his mother was less than approving. Catholicism at that time was considered so far beyond the limits as to not be Christian at all. Catholics swore their loyalty to the Pope, not to Jesus — or so the Baptist reasoning went — and you might as well rotate your head and spew profanities as to be Catholic.

So it was that on March 17, St. Patrick's Day, Sonny and Loretta got married while Edith and Ruth stayed outside the church, showing their disapproval of the union

CHAPTER THREE

Sarah Rose

1898

My grandmother, Sarah Rose Kolakowksi, was born into a world of limitations and hard edges. Born in Russia in 1899, she entered this life in a year that would be remembered globally. Cuba was liberated from Spain that year. War between the Philippines and the United States broke out. In less earthshaking developments, a horse named Manuel won the 25th Kentucky Derby, while Americans danced the bunny hug, the turkey trot and the cakewalk. Among the most popular songs that year were the *Honolulu*

Cakewalk, A Ragtime Skedaddle, and the still-familiar *William Tell Overture.* Some things never age.

It's not likely her parents Adam and Julia Kolakowski did much dancing, having arrived separately in the United States not long before their daughter Sarah was born. Adam had made the trip to the New World alone six months earlier, intending to join his brother Walter on the farm Walter owned near Nanticoke, Pennsylvania. His wife Julia followed some months later, very pregnant with my grandmother Sarah and anxious to make the voyage. She was travelling with their son Billy, who was five years old at the time.

It was a familiar journey that had been made for hundreds of years, by untold thousands of immigrants seeking a new way forward. In 1898, the journey from Poland to America represented a significant chapter in the history of immigration, marked by hope, hardship, and the pursuit of better opportunities. Many Polish immigrants embarked on this voyage driven by economic hardship, political unrest, and the desire for a brighter future. The voyage typically began in ports such as Gdańsk or other Baltic Sea locations, where travelers boarded steamships that would carry them across the Atlantic Ocean. The crossing was often arduous, lasting several weeks, during which passengers endured cramped conditions, limited sanitation, and uncertainty about their destination. Upon arrival in America, many of the newcomers settled in urban centers like New York City, Chicago, and Pittsburgh, where they sought employment in burgeoning industries such as steel, textiles, and construction. The journey was not only a physical transition but also a profound cultural shift, as immigrants faced language barriers, discrimination, and the challenge of maintaining their cultural identity while integrating into American society. Despite these difficulties, the journey from Poland to America in 1898 symbolized resilience and the enduring hope for a new beginning, laying the foundation for future generations of Polish Americans and contributing significantly to the demographic and cultural fabric of the United States.

Coming to grips with life in a new land was too demanding for anything less than hard work and a daily focus on keeping their heads above water. Adam had been enticed to relocate his family from Poland with promises of a better life in America. Brokers from the coal mines would fish for new recruits in Poland, Russia and Ireland, telling them they could come to the United States and have houses, good pay, and dreams limited only by their ambitions. In exchange for these modest riches, they just had to work grueling jobs and long hours for the owners of the mines. It was misleading to say the least. The houses were owned by the mines; everyday basics were sold at the company stores; and the miners themselves were a form of indentured servants. It was a vicious, deliberate circle not unique to mining, but on full display in the towns where they thrived. It seemed that for every dollar a miner was paid, he was somehow charged two more. Getting ahead was as elusive as it's always been, but much more difficult in an era before minimum wages, five-day work weeks, or anything remotely resembling worker safety.

The Kolakowskis couldn't resist the offer and opportunity, so they left their homeland and moved to America. Being as in love as they were made it less daunting. Adam, Julia, and soon their children, were a tightly knit family held together first by the couple's commitment to each other. Where Adam went, Julia went also, determined to travel whatever path life offered them.

No one knows how a family curse begins, or which person will be the one to eventually break it. The Kolakowski curse started in 1898 with the birth of Sarah Rose to her immigrant mother two weeks after she had arrived from Poland. Almost immediately after coming to the New World, Julia's second child was born in a rooming house in Perth Amboy, New Jersey. Told the birth was imminent, Adam quickly made the trip from Nanticoke to meet them there.

After their daughter was safely in the world, they settled in Nanticoke where Adam's older brother Walter owned the farm. Adam fully expected them to be lifelong residents, with his brother and the farm nearby and everything they might want or need available in the well-established mining town.

Not everything was a proverbial bed of roses, or even close to it. Sarah's childhood would be short and marked by upheaval. Survival on the lower end of the socioeconomic scale left little margin for innocence or child's play. Growing up was serious business, and Sarah was thrust into it quickly.

Located in Luzerne County in the Northeastern part of the state, Nanticoke today boasts a population of over 10,000 souls. As with many towns in this area of the country, its name was derived from a Native American word, this one meaning "tidewater." The name was appearing on maps as early as 1776, giving the place a sense of history tied to the nation itself.

Nanticoke became famous for its anthracite coal mining. Also known as hard coal, or black coal, anthracite is most plentiful in Northeastern Pennsylvania, where the largest deposits of it can be found.

Coal mining was generational for a lot of men and their families, and would remain so as long as there were mines to work. It was also a booming industry, decades before anyone was lamenting its passing with the introduction of other forms of energy production. There was no such thing as clean energy, or even the idea of it. Windmills were for railing against like the great Don Quixote. That left coal, and there was enough of it in the ground to burn through the lives of ten thousand miners whose choices were few.

Coal was king, like cotton before it, and Nanticoke was among its great principalities. The joys of coal mining were non-existent, once you factored out the ability to make a modest living, and the sense of community it provided to the miners and their families. At the same time, mining's hazards were plentiful, its consequences often dire, up to and including a shortened life that sometimes ended abruptly. The same year of Sarah's birth, mining had experienced its worst disaster to date in Pennsylvania mining's history. On the morning of December 23, 1899, an explosion at the Braznell Mine in Fayette County resulted in the deaths of 17 miners, making headlines around the country. As catastrophic as that event seemed, it was not the first and wouldn't be the last. Mining is dangerous, dirty, and back-breaking work. Among the risks a miner faces are collapsing mines, explosions, gas poisoning—with or without a dead canary as an early warning system—and heavy machinery accidents. Breathing in coal dust can cause black lung, a dreaded but common disease that can lead to coughing up blood, choking, and very unpleasant death. Miners work countless hours, with little time to spend in the small homes provided by the mining companies. Children were expected to work from a young age at any job available, extending the cycle of subsistence living to the next generation, and the next. Getting ahead or saving for that rainy day was all but impossible on pay that often averaged *.93 cents a day*.

This is the world Adam and Julia Kolakowski exchanged for their life in Poland. It may seem bleak to most people, but to coal miners doing their utmost to make a better life it was the best choice they had. It was also the only world young Sarah knew before it was interrupted by a trip to the orphanage.

***

Catholic orphanages peaked between 1914 and 1920 with the pressures created by unwed parents, immigration, World War I and the deadly influenza pandemic that claimed the lives of many parents. In Luzerne County where more than a dozen orphanages were established, St. Stanislaus was founded to care for children who were casualties in many cases of the times in which they lived. When some of them died they were interred in the orphanage's children's cemetery, where the consequences of a difficult existence were displayed on tombstones. Birth to death, dust to dust, one-stop shopping for the destitute and the abandoned.

Consisting of three interconnected buildings built between 1918 and 1938, St. Stanislaus Orphanage and Holy Child Church was originally intended for use as an orphanage for Polish children. Over the course of its fifty-plus year history, more than 8,000 children found themselves under the care of the Bernadine Sisters of St. Stanislaus. What may be surprising is that many of the children were not actually orphans. Poverty, poor living conditions, and relaxed cultural mores in urban areas helped create a need for these homes, while smaller towns like Nanticoke sometimes relied on religious communities to accommodate the demand for someplace to house these children.

Julia surrendered her daughter to the orphanage for a short time for financial reasons. In the early 1900s, many immigrant families faced significant economic hardships upon arriving in new countries, often due to limited job opportunities, language barriers, and unfamiliar social systems. As a result, some parents resorted to placing their children in orphanages as a strategy to cope with these financial struggles. This decision was frequently driven by the urgent need to make ends meet, where the immediate concern was securing basic necessities such as food, shelter, and safety. Orphanages, which were often run by charitable organizations or religious institutions, provided a form of temporary relief, offering children shelter and care while their families attempted to stabilize their economic situation. Additionally, some families believed that orphanages could provide better educational opportunities and a more stable environment for their children than what they could afford at home. However, this practice also reflected the harsh realities faced by immigrant families, including poverty, social exclusion, and the lack of support systems, which compelled them to make difficult decisions in the hope of securing a better future for their children. Over time, these practices contributed to broader discussions about child welfare, social support, and the responsibilities of society to assist vulnerable populations during periods of economic hardship.

Sarah was a beautiful baby, healthy and good, but she had a fiery side to her. A lively child, she was sent off to the orphanage when she was 10 years old. Sarah retuned home at the age of 12. By then she was a skilled seamstress, taught by the orphanage, with a passion for her work. One day there was a fire in the house where Sarah and her parents lived. As the fire alarm rang out her family escaped. Sarah rushed back into the house to save a bolt of fabric she'd been working with. Had it not been for the intervention of a volunteer fireman named Joseph Kaminski, she may well have perished as human kindling. That fireman and Sarah's 's fates would soon become entwined.

Joseph rushed into the house, performing his fireman's duties, and saved the girl inside. As grateful as Sarah was to survive, it was not the fairytale rescue it may seem. Joseph was a hardscrabble entrepreneur, not a prince saving a damsel in distress.

Joseph was a coal miner at the time of the fire. The wages weren't nearly enough for anything more than treading water. Joseph was not a treader, so he'd opened a gambling establishment that also operated as a bar and a brothel—a small but significant boost to his standard of living. Satiating the appetites of the men in town provided a steady stream of customers.

When Sarah woke up later in the hospital—a rare accommodation at a time when hospitals were for people of means—she found Joseph sitting at her bedside stroking her hair. It's possible he had paid for the hospital, given the expense of it. Whether or not he'd asked for repayment, either for covering the cost or simply saving the girl's life, Sarah's mother showed her gratitude by giving him her daughter's hand in marriage. Joseph was 25, Sarah was 13.

Marriage was not a negotiation. Children in those times weren't asked what their preferences were or if they were in love with the person they'd been told to marry. Parents often arranged these things and sometimes still do, through pressures and expectations. For Sarah it was not a question, and there was only one right answer if it had been. She obeyed her parents, and in short order she became a thirteen-year-old bride: Mrs. Joseph Kaminski, soon to be a teenage mother, survivor of a house fire, girl seamstress, and, on her wedding night, a sexual assault victim. Joseph, as far from being a hero as he could be, barred their bedroom door with a dresser and took what he'd expected to be given. If she resisted, it would be taken by force. Sarah Kaminski did not resist.

Sarah Rose was but a child herself, hardly a woman, when she was forcibly entered on the eve of her wedding by a man she barely knew. She endured his will, and his power, and the end of her innocence, when all she wanted to do was go home to play with her dolls.

A short nine months later, Sarah gave birth to her first child. Sadly, he was stillborn, because her body had not matured enough to carry another living soul into the world. Sarah went into a deep depression, unimaginable for a 14-year-old, and in the spring she discovered she was pregnant again. This time she delivered a healthy baby girl who she loved like she'd loved her doll babies that she had left at her mother's home. Little Helen was sweet and pretty, and she gave her mother endless delight.

Now Sarah had a child to care for and play with, but fate was not kind. Helen died in her mother's arms from pneumonia shortly after her second birthday.

Sarah eventually found herself at the age of eighteen, having already given birth to two children whose lives had been snuffed out so shortly. She ultimately had five children with Joseph, including the two she'd lost. Her grief was not bearable for someone twice her age, yet she survived it, taking it into her soul with the memories of the children she'd lost when she was barely an adult herself. It was a crucible that shaped her and strengthened her for the rest of her life.

CHAPTER FOUR

End of Innocence

1915 – 1921

It was a time when women and children had no legal agency of their own, when they were considered a form of property belonging to their husbands, fathers and brothers. Women would not have the right to vote until 1919 with the passage of the 19th Amendment, ratified a year later. They could not own homes or acquire credit of any kind, and women without men to claim them were often left to fend for themselves in a world where the odds were against them.

Well before any of the incremental rights we take for granted today, Sarah had already passed through her childhood into motherhood with nothing in-between. She had been married off to a man who was unconcerned with her happiness, in a society that gave little consideration to what girls and women wanted. Sarah found herself staring at a headstone with the name of her stillborn son's name on it.

"When I was a child, I spoke as a child, I understood as a child, I thought as a child: but when I became a man, I put away childish things."

1st Corinthian 13:11 instructs readers to put away the things of the child. Sarah was forced to do this as she became a woman living in a man's world. It was the only one available to her.

Sarah became pregnant again the following spring, this time with a healthy baby girl she named Helen. She quickly learned that a real baby is not the same as a make-believe one

The child mortality rate in the United States when Helen was born was approximately 185 deaths per 1,000 live births for children under five years old. Among the main diseases claiming them were infectious illnesses like tuberculosis, pneumonia, and influenza, along with heart disease. Helen contracted pneumonia at the age of two, an even more life-threatening illness at the time than it is now. Antibiotics would not be invented until the 1920s and 30s, and penicillin was unheard of until 1928. For a child her age it proved insurmountable, and it claimed Helen's young life at the age of two. Sarah was inconsolable, holding the girl in her arms as she gasped her last breath. It was an emotional cataclysm that sent Sarah into a depression with nowhere to turn, no one to help her through it. It's easy to forget how few resources were available then, from modern medicines to any sort of therapy or emotional support. Those things were unheard of, and the demands of daily living required Sarah to grieve privately and quickly. She would have to carry her sorrow inside herself. Life moved on at an unsettling speed for a time we often mistakenly think was slower. (What we've come to call modern conveniences are only that; they didn't replace all the things that needed to be done day-to-day.)

Joseph took the losses with a certain stride bordering on indifference. They were part of their existence. Life really was quick and brutal for most people, especially those without the means to stave off its inevitable consequences. Joseph was preoccupied attempting to acquire those means. He had other things to focus on besides the common loss of children, specifically his businesses. By the time his second child died he'd established his thriving gambling den that did triple duty as a bar and a brothel. Sarah tended to the thirsty patrons, filling their glasses and taking their coin, well aware of the activities around her. If she had moral reservations about the gambling and the prostitution they were not expressed — opinions were for men to have, not women. She also continued to perform her marital duties, a euphemism for keeping her husband sexually satisfied, and when she was 18 she gave birth to a strong son, Stanley Kaminski. Would this time be different?

Would God allow her to keep this child past his infancy?

A slender, quiet boy, Stanley proved to be resilient. He gave his mother years of pleasure and pride, growing into adulthood and eventually serving his country in the military. He would remain a quiet, unassuming man all his days.

As the river of her life continued to wind its way, Sarah gave birth at the age of 19 ½ to Irene, a daughter who would also survive into adulthood and have her own child some years later. Now with two healthy children, Sarah did her best to pour her love into Stanley and Irene. It was not something Joseph reciprocated, if in fact love had ever existed between them. He was too busy with his modest empire to pay attention to his wife and children.

One day while Sarah was pushing Irene in her baby carriage, running errands or taking the child and herself out for some air, she heard a whistle from across the street. She turned and saw a young man waving at her. He appeared to be one of the many coal miners in town, and decidedly good-looking. He wasn't short, stumpy and much older than her like Joseph, but tall and thin. He was also handsome to a degree that could be seen across a street. As he came toward her, he displayed an exuberance and a forwardness that startled her. She stopped the carriage and waited as he hurried over to where she stood. And in that chance encounter she met a stranger who would not remain unknown to her for long. His kindness, his looks, and his heart quickly captured

Sarah Rose, and for the first and only time in her life she fell in love.

Sarah didn't know in that moment she was looking into the eyes of the man who would become the love of her life. His name was Alex Naguszweksi, unmistakably Polish like nearly everyone in her life. He'd been surprisingly forward, which may have been the only way their stars would have crossed. Had he not been brazen, her life story and the stories of her descendants would all be different. The interest he expressed that day was mutual, quickly developing into a relationship that would change everything.

CHAPTER FIVE

Say a Little Prayer

1921 – 1924

Stories like that of Sarah Rose and other Polish migrants have been told in North America since 1608, long before it was the United States. Following their earliest presence on the continent there have been three great waves of migration. The first and largest lasted from 1870 to 1914, covering the time Adam and Julia Kolakowski arrived. A second wave followed World War II, as millions sought escape from a shattered Europe, and a third after Poland's regime change in 1989. The adjustment to a new country and culture wasn't easy. Up to a third of Poles living in the United States repatriated to Poland within a few years, finding the changes too daunting or simply missing the land of their roots, but the majority stayed and did their best to thrive. High wages and plentiful jobs for unskilled labor enticed the immigrants to make the journey, uncertain of a future but hoping for the best. American mining, meatpacking, construction, steelwork, and heavy industry offered a path to renewal after the hardships of their homeland. Most Poles settled into communities with other Polish immigrants. The largest and possibly most famous is in Chicago, but it was by no means the only one.

The coal mines of Pennsylvania also beckoned with promises of homes and a less grueling existence, all of which turned out to be only partially true. While an improvement over the hardships many of them faced in Poland, the miner's lives required back-breaking work and extreme perseverance. This is the world the hopeful immigrants entered and where most, including Adam, Julia and their descendants, would remain. For a significant majority, there was no going back.

Having introduced themselves during a chance encounter on a street in Nanticoke, Sarah and Alex hesitantly decided they should meet again. It would need to be clandestine, given the cultural restrictions of a disapproving society. It may not have been love at first sight, but it had caused an undeniable spark between them. It was obvious to Alex that this beautiful woman was married — she was there with a child in a carriage — but that didn't stop him. The impulse to know more about her had been too great to be tempered by moral constraints.

Sarah informed the brash young man that she went to church every day, observing mass as a good Catholic would. The conversation would have been clear but discreet: they were exchanging pleasantries on a sidewalk, should anyone notice. Even under the circumstances she quickly thought about her options. Not seeing him again wasn't one of them. She suggested Alex meet her for the 6:00 AM service the next morning. There was nothing inappropriate about going to mass — there might be eternal consequences to skipping it. Her husband would not be joining her, as he seldom did. Alex agreed, feigning reluctance, and their next meeting was set.

The next morning Alex followed Sarah into the church and sat beside her as they solemnly observed the service. There weren't many people at the early mass, but they both knew prying eyes might invite people's curiosity. Sarah fingered her beads and said her rosary, being sure to include a prayer that involved the man sitting next to her. She had spent the rest of the day and night before preparing herself for the possibilities. If this was God's will, who could object? And if if wasn't, she would take her chances.

By the time mass was finished, Sarah knew she could not deny the feelings she felt blossoming for Alex. It was unfamiliar to her after being shackled to Joseph. She had known responsibility, motherhood, and a premature adulthood, but she had not known love. She wasn't even sure if this was it, but it felt like nothing she'd experienced before except for the love of her family and her children. She decided not to deny her own desires for the first time in her life.

They continued to meet secretly at different places and times, careful not to expose themselves to a scandal. They were also determined to remain chaste. This was not technically adultery, and neither of them would allow anything physical to happen beyond their intense desire for each other. Divorce was considered a mortal sin by the Church, and not something to be contemplated lightly, if at all. On the other hand, the couple knew they had to be together eventually, no matter what was required or how high the price would be. They both knew there was a life expectancy to what they were experiencing, and putting it off for another day could mean that day never came.

One morning the town's whistle blared through the sky. Everyone knew what it meant: there had been an accident at the coal mine. Sometimes these were explosions, sometimes they were fires, and often they were both. A cave-in rarely came with a warning. A deep crack, the ground shuddering, then instant darkness as lamps were crushed by tons of coal and rock collapsing in seconds. Buried alive, trapped in pockets of air, surrounded by silence broken only by the groans of the men left alive. In the silence there was the slow dripping of water. Breathing became the first battle. Gas was now leaking. Coal dust filled their lungs. Oxygen thinned. Some men were scratching messages into timbers and walls, praying someone would find their last message to loved ones.

The townspeople all dropped what they were doing, and as one community they rushed to the mine.

One of the the most terrifying events a community could have, it unfolded in minutes underground, then stretched into days and weeks above ground, changing families forever. The waiting game begins.

Sarah gathered her children and dashed off with the others. Unbeknownst to anyone else, her primary concern was not for her husband, who was also in the mine that day. She was desperate to find out if anything had happened to Alex. It was one of the times in her life when she believed God had heard and answered her prayers — both Alex and Joseph were among the survivors. Church doors were opened, women cooked large pots of food for everyone who waited anxiously for news. Neighbors watched children whose parents stood at the mine day and night. Priests moved through the crowds praying with families. Time slowed to a standstill. If rescue was attempted, volunteer miners went back underground. Men risked their own lives to save their friends and brothers. They listened for knocking sounds, and silence brought no hope. Children remembered their mothers crying, seeing men come home covered in dust or not coming home at all, learning very young that the mine could take a father without warning. A coal mine cave-in didn't just trap men underground. It shattered an entire community.

Sarah was relieved beyond words that Alex and their future together were still possible. He emerged from the mine shaken but unharmed. It was then they decided the time had come. She could not live without Alex, and he could not live without her.

She went into confession the next day and admitted to the priest, who may have been aware of the rumors, that she had feelings for Alex. The priest told her to say 10 Hail Marys and ask God to take this desire from her. Surrendering to it was unthinkable to the priest, and divorce was out of the question. It was not, however, out of the question for Sarah. After having been forced into a marriage when she was still a girl, she wouldn't be thwarted in her own happiness.

Having narrowly escaped death in a coal mine, Alex determined to secure his future with Sarah. One night he went striding into Joseph's saloon. Sarah was tending bar and was startled to see him. He had never done that before, but he entered with a sense of mission to do whatever was necessary for a life with the woman he loved. He approached Joseph and asked to speak to him privately in the back room. Sarah stayed busy but kept one eye on the doorway, wondering what could be happening. She never knew exactly what was said, but the men had come to an arrangement. That was very much in character for Joseph, who had not loved his wife and who saw a possible transaction in almost every encounter.

The deal became clear soon enough when Alex went to work for Joseph for the next three years. It was a way to essentially buy Sarah's freedom: a trade of labor and time for the emancipation of his soul mate. Sarah was neither hurt nor surprised that Joseph would agree to this. He may have been an unloving man, at least toward her, but he was also reasonable. He likely realized that setting Sarah free would in some ways free himself. But first there was a debt to pay.

Sarah remained in her marriage to Joseph during this time, still performing her wifely and motherly duties while Alex kept his end of the bargain. It was an agreement made all the more intense by their insistence on not crossing a line they'd set for themselves: sexual intimacy would have to wait.

Alex went back to work at the coal mine at 5:00 AM. Earing a living in the in the Pennsylvania coal mines meant sacrificing your body for your family's survival. The threat of danger was constant, and holding onto your dignity through the community, required faith and resilience.

He came out of the mine by 4:00 PM and went to work at Joseph's saloon until 2:00 AM, with nothing to fuel him between shifts but a quick bath and a piece of bread.

It was an excruciatingly long three years for them both. The only thing that makes time move more slowly than youth is youth in love. Finally the day had come, with or without the Church's or society's approval. Alex had fulfilled his obligation to work for Joseph and he was released from his commitment. To complicate matters, Sarah was pregnant again with Joseph's third child. In keeping with an already surprisingly pragmatic situation, Joseph did not resist his pregnant wife's leaving with Alex. The gentlemen's agreement between the men had been completed, and Alex was content to raise the child who would now be theirs. A quick divorce was arranged for Sarah and Joseph. An annulment from the Catholic church was never granted, so Alex and Sarah could never receive communion again.

In 1924, in a simple wedding at Town Hall, Sarah and Alex married at last. It wasn't fancy like Sarah's first arranged marriage to Joseph Kaminski. This time it was for love, and little else was needed or wanted. Not long afterward Sarah gave birth to Joseph's child, whom she named Helen in honor of her deceased daughter. Alex stepped in as a father and taking care of them both. They enjoyed their little family so much they added two more children of their own to the flock, my mother Loretta in 1928, and her sister Gerri in 1933.

All was well for some years, with the girls enjoying their childhood while their parents made a life for the family. Then the circus came to town.

CHAPTER SIX

Under the Big Tent

1924 – 1938

Alex and Sarah settled into their own home in Nanticoke, Pennsylvania, with their growing family. Joseph and Sarah's daughter, also named Helen, was born in 1924, blessing them with a healthy baby at last. The little girl was another child Sarah could care for and enjoy. Sarah would take in sewing jobs to earn money, while Alex continued to work in the mines for many years to come.

The couple went on to have Loretta in 1928, and Geraldine in 1933. Life was hard, but it was also wonderful. They still had their other growing children who had stayed with Joseph Kaminski, and who they visited from time to time — they lived just several blocks away. They would all meet and go to mass together on Sundays. After service they would head to the town square so the men could play checkers in the afternoon while the children played games. Life seemed simple then. There was always just enough money to go around. Loretta adored her father Alex, and she was somewhat of a tomboy at the time. She's told me stories about walking down by the railroad tracks in the winter with a bucket to pick up pieces of coal that had fallen off the train so they could come home and keep the house warm. It was ironic when you think about it: Alex working in the mines during the day, then waiting for discarded handouts to heat the house. Loretta was sent to clean the front porch of the neighbors' houses for .5 cents, and everyone in the family worked to keep them all going. Yet no one complained.

Then one day the circus came to town.

For most people, having the circus and its caravan of entertainments show up nearby evokes childhood memories of elephants, clowns and cotton candy. But for some who lived in the early part of the 20th century, the circus had less appealing undertones, especially for children who found themselves sold to the Big Tent.

It's difficult for people today to imagine such a thing, but it was not uncommon and not all that shocking for a family to sell or lend a child to a travelling circus. The most notable instances involved children who suffered with physical deformities and found themselves being gawked at behind curtains where admission was charged to view them as living oddities. Others were kidnapped or sold into servitude within the circus industry itself, sometimes being traded from one circus to another.

In these ways the circus was not only a source of diversion for communities, but also a complex and sometimes troubling facet of American society at the time. Traveling circuses proliferated and some children became victims of exploitation within this industry. Part of this was caused by the economic hardships following the Great Depression of 1929 – 1939 that left many families in desperate situations. The Great Depression was a severe global economic downturn. The period was characterized by high rates of unemployment and poverty. Reductions in industrial production and international trade, with widespread bank and business failures around the world, made it extremely difficult for most people.

Some parents felt pressured to sell their children to these circuses, either from financial difficulties or even the allure of adventure and recognition. The term "stage mother" took on new meaning when it was the mother of a circus child seeking vicarious fame and fortune through a son or daughter who would not protest too loudly.

Children who became part of the circus often kept to grueling schedules and endured harsh conditions. They performed in acts ranging from acrobatics to animal taming, and the demands placed on them could be far more rigorous than any child should experience.

Public awareness of the practice began to grow during the late 1920s, with advocacy groups calling attention to the plight of these children. Circus recruitment and the treatment of child performers began to evolve, with many circuses adapting to the rising awareness and changing social attitudes.

It was not all that unusual when Sarah sold Loretta to a circus that had set up tent in Scranton. Young Loretta was blessed with an exceptional singing voice that could be heard throughout the house. Sarah saw — and heard — an opportunity to make use of that talent by offering her daughter to work as a vocalist. It's almost certain she considered this a temporary situation, a transaction that exchanged Loretta and her voice for a cash payment and a continued income the child could send home. Loretta had always been a good daughter, loving and faithful to a fault. When informed she would be working for the circus she did as her mother told her, going to work at a job where she literally sang for her supper among the clowns and animal trainers.

Traveling circuses were famous across the nation, bringing amusements and illusions to communities that anticipated their visits the way a dry spell waits for rain. Arriving during the summer months, the circus drew crowds to local fairgrounds or parks where they would set up operations. Advertisements filled the newspapers, colorful posters thrilling everyone with depictions of daring acrobats, exotic creatures and endless spectacle. Families made a day of it, spending hours strolling through midway games and eating food from a dozen vendors all vying for their attention. And for a time they enjoyed the sweet sound of Loretta's voice, performing on a schedule and impressing the paying customers.

Circuses also had a less apparent sense of danger to them: maybe the lion tamer would lose his head to the lion. Or the sword swallower might aim his sword a little too far to one side and send the audience screaming from the bleachers. There were also dangers the public remained unaware of, particularly the risk of fire. Given all the fabric, wooden poles, and straw spread out for the animals, the tents were highly vulnerable to flames. Made of cotton and treated with paraffin to waterproof them, they could easily ignite and be engulfed by fire within minutes.

Loretta and her parents were as unaware of the dangers as the people who came to the circus to be dazzled and delighted for a few hours. It was during a show shortly after Loretta had begun performing that a fire broke out in one of the tents. While the fire didn't consume the circus and no one was seriously hurt, it was enough to make Alex hurry to Scranton and remove his daughter from such a hazardous job and life.

It remains unclear what conversation Alex and Sarah had about it all. Sarah had handed their daughter over to the circus in an effort to raise money for the family, and Alex had retrieved her almost as quickly. The episode provided one of the more unusual pieces to the puzzle of Loretta's life.

CHAPTER SEVEN

Betrayal of Innocence

1940

The early years of Loretta and Geraldine's lives had been nearly idyllic, circus tents and fires aside. They spent summers at their Uncle Walter's large farm, swimming and skipping stones across the lake. The girls also pitched in with the never-ending work a farm requires, dutifully performing whatever chores they were given, including milking the cows.

Milk was kept cool in the days before widespread refrigeration by storing it below ground in a cellar or basement. Uncle Walter stored the cows' milk in a cistern where spring water filled up the tank and kept barrels of milk cool. Loretta was sometimes sent downstairs to scoop milk into containers and bring it back up for the family.

One morning she went to the cistern and found something other than milk waiting for her. Uncle Walter followed her down and came quickly up behind her. She was too young to know anything about sex other than what she saw naturally among the farm animals.

This kind of trauma of a young girl is often called betrayal trauma. It effects how a child's brain, identity, and self develop, shattering a sense of safety. When the harm comes from a family member, someone who is supposed to protect the child, she learns the world is not safe: people who love her can hurt her. This often leads to chronic anxiety. Because the abuser is someone familiar, the child learns that love and pain are connected. Saying no doesn't matter. The child has difficulty accepting love when it's genuine, and memory gaps develop. The most important truth may be that the damage happens because of the betrayal, not because of anything the child did. The child cannot stop the abuse, and doesn't cause the adult's wrong doing.

Finding herself being treated this way had to have been devastating. It was also a variation on a theme familiar to women and girls the world over. Her mother Sarah had been assaulted when she was not much older than Loretta by the man she'd been forced to marry. And now it was Loretta's turn in a horrible repetition that travels with grim predictability from one generation to the next.

The world Loretta knew was forever changed, having had her eyes opened to the casual brutality and indifference of some men. It was a shock to her physically and emotionally, and she couldn't hide it from her parents. In some ways she was not the same girl after that, and they knew it.

It was decades before abuse of this kind was reported to any authorities. Even now children are not always believed, and the perpetrators can sometimes go on for years without detection or any real danger of exposure. What mattered was that Alex knew his brother had violated his daughter, and remaining there was not an option. His family was all that mattered to him. In a move whose true motives would only be spoken of privately, Alex and Sarah decided to take the family to Newark, New Jersey, and begin yet again.

***

With the depression waning and war raging across Europe and Asia, Alex began to see the writing on the wall. The small town of Nanticoke offered little opportunity beyond the mines, the saloons, and the farms that stretch endlessly toward the horizon. He was ambitious, determined to create a life that matched the size of his dreams, not the narrow limitations imposed by geography or circumstance. Every detail of their lives seemed to converge at the right moment, pointing toward a single solution: move, and move decisively.

Newark, New Jersey, was a vibrant city in the late 1930s and early 1940s, known for its industries and thriving communities. It had the advantages of being a strategic transportation hub, bustling with factories and warehouses, all served by a major port just a stone's throw from New York City. Industries that fueled Newark's economy included pharmaceuticals, machinery, and food processing. As war escalated in Europe, the city's industrial base shifted toward military production, creating jobs and attracting workers from far and wide, including many like Alex and Sarah who came with high hopes and a willingness for hard work. The move offered them a way forward. It also removed them from Walter's farm and the trauma Loretta had endured.

Having arranged for Sarah's two older children with Joseph to remain with him, they packed up their belongings, and with their three young girls, Helen, Loretta and Gerri, they made the big move.

There had always been an abundance of laughter and love in the Naszweksi household. Despite the trauma Loretta was subjected to by her uncle, their new start in a big city was as exciting as it was daunting. Alex and Sarah would need to find work, which they quickly did. They also needed housing, and within a short time they had moved into a 10-story walk up cold water flat on Springfield Avenue. Defined by their lack of running hot water, cold water flats were common in Newark in the 1940s and 50s. The tenants in these flats were required to make their own heat and hot water using the stove.

The building was unique in its triangular shape, and gleamed with slick white tiles throughout. More than just a new home for the families living there, it was like the United Nations, with different languages and the smells of food from their native countries wafting through everyone's doors. The Italians making gravy with garlic and basil, tomato sauce simmering on the stove. When you walked up another flight you smelled kielbasa and sauerkraut from the Polish homes. All the scents would intensify in the summer heat with no air conditioning and very few screens on the windows. After a Sunday meal, people would congregate on the building's rooftop overlooking the city of Newark. They would bring their blankets and homemade wine to share with their neighbors, sustaining the small community they'd made for themselves. These evenings on the roof helped them all feel as if they'd succeeded in their new country, and good things would surely follow.

***

The city below the rooftops was always bustling, with saloons on nearly every corner and a public transportation system that included trolleys on tracks and buses on streets, some of which were still cobblestone. They were unlike anything the family had seen before. In the early 1940s Newark's trolleys were a vital part of its public transportation network, providing essential services to residents and visitors. The system included various trolley routes that connected neighborhoods to downtown Newark and the surrounding communities, making the daily routine of its people possible. The trolleys were also affordable and convenient, providing easy access to schools, workplaces, and local businesses.

Times were so different then for the country. With war still on, cities like Newark mandated blackouts in the evenings to shield them from attacks by the air. All lights were turned off, dark shades were pulled down over the windows. Military, police and emergency vehicles had their headlights half-blacked out. Newark had one of the best United Service Organizations (USO) locations, its version of the Hollywood Cantina. It was a place where young ladies could relax and dance with elegant uniformed men on leave, enjoying a night at the Continental Ballroom on Broad Street.

Newark offered several opportunities for outdoor activity, community and amusement. Among the most popular was Olympic Park, which the family soon discovered to their delight. Opened in 1904 under its new name, the park had previously been called Hilton Park. Intended to compete with Electric Park, where visitors could thrill to the sorts of attractions they'd find at New York's Coney Island, the park was renamed in honor of the Olympic Games held that year in St Louis. Its new entrance was designed to impress, with four huge pillars and an electrified sign flashing the park's name overhead. Just beyond the front gate were two large lion statues, while over two thousand electric lights illuminated the park's midway at night.

The midway was something to see, featuring a 20-foot-high Helter-Skelter spiral slide, a Moorish palace-style fun house, swings, gypsy fortune tellers, and camel and pony rides for the children. There was an immense dancing pavilion that could accommodate hundreds of excited dancers, many of them out for a romantic evening. Management's emphasis was on family attractions that appealed to every age group. Space at the old baseball field was allotted to the circus, which was booked for the entire season.

The Park was also home to an enormous swimming pool that was among its most spectacular attractions. The pool was 400 feet long and 200 feet wide with a depth ranging from 9-

1/2 feet to less than a foot. It required 3,750,000 gallons of filtered chlorinated water, and could accommodate 4,000 bathers at one time.

The carousel, another main attraction that provided a lifetime of memories, eventually ended up being moved to Disney World.

The 1940s were transformational for the park, as economic prosperity and a desire for leisure activities drew ever-larger crowds. It remained a cherished part of Newark's history until it closed in 1965, but when the Naguszweksis arrived it was in its prime.

For young Helen, Loretta and Geraldine, it was as if they'd entered a fantastic world where trolleys crisscrossed the city, giant parks teemed with people and surprises and even giraffes. So many things seemed magical, but like magic of all kinds there were secrets yet to be revealed.

CHAPTER EIGHT

Photo Booth and Bridges

1941

Alex knew for every hour of pleasure there would need to be ten more of work, and he quickly found a job with the state. In 1941, workers across New Jersey were employed painting bridges as part of the The Works Progress Administration (WPA), a pivotal New Deal agency established in the 1930s by President Franklin D. Roosevelt. Its primary objective was to combat the widespread unemployment caused by the Great Depression. The WPA played a crucial role in constructing roads, bridges, schools, hospitals, and other public facilities across the United States.

Alex's co-workers included skilled painters like himself who coated the bridges' steel with special paint to make sure the structures could withstand the elements. The job was labor-intensive, requiring Alex and the others to use scaffolding and harnesses in work that occasionally cost one of the men their lives.

Sarah, too, did her part, eventually finding a job making batteries at RCA. She was always on the lookout for other ways to supplement their income, and she had always been a keen observer of people and their desires. It may have been seeing the fortune tellers at Olympic Park that encouraged her to take up Tarot card reading as a side job. She couldn't help noticing how many people — women especially — would hand over portions of their family budget to hear some version of what they already believed. She studied them, and in short time became a respected card reader herself. Sometimes she was paid in cash, other times in fruits and vegetables.

One of the most common things women wanted to know was the well-being of their sons at war. Hand-written correspondence was the only effective means of communication at the time. It created an anticipation hard to imagine in today's world of texting and video calls. The postal service was a singular lifeline between families and their sons defending Western civilization in foreign lands. Parents fretted daily, hoping the mailman would bring them proof their sons were alive, and the sons knew few pleasures as great as getting letters from home. But the system was sluggish and flawed, with an excruciating lag time that could leave a mother and father without word for months or even years. It created a monumental backlog of mail for the military that defied solution, until, near the end of the war, America's only all-Black, all-female battalion was assigned the task. It was assumed they would fail, since every effort before them had not conquered the mountains of mail left idling in hundreds of bags stored in hangars. They were wrong. The 6888th Central Postal Directory Battalion (known as the Six Triple Eight), was given the job with no expectation of success. The Battalion's leader, Major Charity Adams, was the first African-American woman to become an officer in the Women's Army Auxiliary Corps (WACs). Leading her group of tireless women who had been instilled with her own fierce commitment, she overcame the odds against them, including the doubts of a hostile commanding officer. He'd given them six months, and they accomplished their mission in less than 90 days.

Until that herculean feat, families had lived with the anxiety of not hearing from their sons for long stretches of time. One unorthodox solution for some of the mothers was found with those midway fortune tellers offering visions revealed to them on Tarot cards.

It's unlikely any of these women were told their cherished boy had died riddled with shrapnel. A fortune teller who was not comforting wouldn't be in business long.

None of this is to say the card readers didn't believe in the futures they saw. It's possible they considered themselves blessed with second sight, and Sarah may have been among them. But what she knew with certainty was that she was skilled at it, and she could please a worried mother while being paid for it at the same time.

Among the other people living in the Springfield Avenue house was an Italian family by the name of Lucadamo, consisting of the Lucadamo parents and their nine children. Mother Gilda had made Sarah's acquaintance on the rooftop when neighbors had gathered together in the summer evenings. Gilda was especially concerned at the time with her son, Oreste, whom everyone called Lucky. He'd been in the service for four years. Being a first-generation immigrant, Gilda spoke little English, but she knew about Sarah's reputation with a deck of Tarot cards. It wasn't unusual when she began to ask Sarah for readings, with the desire to find out about Lucky. Gilda was anxious to know that he was still alive and as safe as a soldier could be fighting a war overseas.

Sarah read Gilda's cards and assured her Lucky was alive and well. As evidence of her fortune telling skills, Lucky came home on leave—proving to his mother's mind that the cards had spoken the truth. Whether his mother ever told him about Sarah's fortune telling talent is a mystery, but it wasn't long before Sarah's daughter Loretta caught his eye and kept it.

One day, after his return, he took the fourteen-year-old Loretta with him and some of his brothers and sisters to celebrate his homecoming. They headed to Olympic Park for an afternoon of fun along the midway. There was a Photo Booth, and Lucky asked Loretta, who was nineteen years younger than himself, to take pictures with him. This was a big deal for people at the time — there were no cell phones to snap selfies with. Invented in 1924, the Photo Booth required sitting in a curtained-off booth, smiling for a camera, and waiting for the negatives to develop. The cost was a whopping $0.25, and would provide a strip of eight black-and-white photos that took eight minutes to develop. It wasn't the kind of instant gratification people later became accustomed to as technology spun us all faster and faster, but the pleasure of seeing yourself posing for the camera was worth every second of waiting.

Lucky cut out one of the photos from the strip and carried it in his wallet for decades after that day. It wasn't long after their trip to the park that the Lucadamos bought their own house on Ninth Avenue in Newark and moved out, maintaining close ties to some of the families they'd shared their lives with on Springfield Avenue. Loretta took to visiting the Lucadamos and babysitting the youngest children for years to come, becoming a welcome fixture in their home, especially for Lucky.

CHAPTER NINE

Easy Living

1948

Air conditioning was a luxury unknown to most people in 1940. Like television, it was something more affluent families were able to enjoy. For everyone else there were front stoops, window fans and rooftops.

Among the neighbors Loretta met during her evenings on the roof was a young woman named Helen Henry. Helen was 19 at the time, five years older than Loretta, and the two took an immediate liking to each other. They shared stories about their lives, as neighbors would do when passing the time together. Helen eventually introduced Loretta to Gene, her boyfriend and hoped-for future husband. After getting to know Loretta, she asked the younger girl if she would act as a chaperone for them. It was common then for young people to be accompanied on anything remotely resembling a date, whether it was out on the town or at home where a watchful eye could be kept over them. This was especially true for Eastern European immigrants, who would not think of allowing their daughters to be alone with a young man. Human nature has never really changed, and parents were keenly aware of the temptations invited by too much privacy. More than a few had fallen prey to them in their own younger days.

Loretta asked for and received permission from her parents to serve as a chaperone for Helen and Gene. The couple didn't question their parents' insistence on having a third person escort them — rules were rules — and soon Loretta was going everywhere with them. It was a relationship that would last a lifetime.

Loretta looked older than her age, which served the threesome well when they went to local taverns, some of which had been speakeasies during Prohibition. From 1920 to 1933, the Eighteenth Amendment to the United States Constitution prevented the sale and production of alcohol nation-wide. This did not stop Americans from drinking. Far from it. Prohibition created a thriving, lucrative, and often deadly black market that gave rise to figures such as Al Capone other famous gangsters and bootleggers, and at least a few politicians. To all appearances drinking was forbidden, but in reality people found a myriad of ways around it. One of them was the establishment and popularity of speakeasies, which were bars carefully hidden from the authorities. People could gain entrance to one of these underground establishments and enjoy live music by entertainers such as Louis "Satchmo" Armstrong, when he wasn't performing at Harlem's famous Cotton Club. The term "speakeasy" may have derived from the requirement of patrons to speak softly through a small opening in the bar's door to gain entrance, with or without a password.

By the time Loretta was going out on the town with Helen and Gene the speakeasies were long gone, reverting to the bars and taverns everyone had known before the Prohibition era. Loretta had no trouble getting in with the older couple. She had a wonderful singing voice and loved to share it with the saloon patrons from time to time, just as she'd sung when she'd been sold to the circus. This time it was only for pleasure, and between her good looks and her powerful voice, the 16-year-old who looked 20 was often the highlight of the evening.

Between her new friends, her new life in Newark, and the newfound freedoms she had, Loretta was experiencing some of the happiest years of her life. The big city had proved to be a welcome change for her. She was mature for her age and highly intelligent, having endured so much as a girl. She loathed the nuns and soon quit the school. With her parents' approval, she found a job with her mother at RCA. She loved the job and the sense of being an adult it gave her. And when she wasn't working, she often spent time as the chaperone for Helen and Gene. It gave her a social life, allowing her to expand her activities and meet so many interesting people. Newark was a long way from a mining town in Pennsylvania, a destination she hadn't imagined before she'd arrived.

On her trips to the Lucadamo's new home to babysit, Lucky would sometimes be there. His romantic fixation on the teenager deepened, and from time to time he would tell her he loved her. Their age difference was unmistakable, and for many years Loretta dismissed his professions of love. She initially saw him as more of an overly affectionate uncle who attempted to demonstrate his fondness by buying her small items of jewelry now and then. One time when he was on a trip to Paris he even had a portrait made of her from a photograph, then presented it to her when he returned. As much as these were the gestures of a paramour, the feelings were not mutual, and Loretta accepted the gifts as politely as she could without encouraging him — something Lucky appeared not to need.

***

Loretta's life continued this way, seemingly fuller every day. Then, one afternoon, she was walking in town when she heard that fateful whistle from across the street. She turned and saw the sailor waving at her, then dashing between cars to the sidewalk where she stood smiling at him. She'd been many things in her life, but naïve was not one of them. The man who was about to introduce himself as George "call me Sonny" Hlopak was not there to ask for directions.

Sonny was tall dark and handsome, with the kindest eyes Loretta had ever seen—not like the older men who had physically molested her, or a man like Lucky who had showered his attentions on her despite their age difference. Here was someone closer to her age in a crisp, white Navy uniform. His gentle manner was immediately evident, and it was what attracted her first. He was intelligent, exhibiting a sense of class without the practiced snobbery money often creates. He knew how to treat a lady, and a lady is what Loretta wanted to be, not some used-up woman whose youth had been stolen from her. Cupid's arrow struck with lightening speed, and within days Loretta and Sonny were an item.

The new couple, Sonny and Loretta, befriended Gene and Helen, and the four of them became inseparable. The men realized immediately that they shared a lust for life, and an entrepreneurial spirit that served as the basis for a lifelong friendship. Loretta and Helen became like sisters, and the four of them were soon bonded. All of this developed under the watchful eye of an unhappy Lucky.

Then one day Loretta received a letter from Sonny. It set the tone for how Sonny felt about this stunning beauty, and how completely he gave her his heart. Loretta shared his emotions, the first time she knew what falling in love felt like.

February 14, 1944

Hello darling, it's early morning and I can't sleep. I've been thinking about you all night. First I need to tell you that it feels so good to call someone darling and really mean it. I know we've know each other just a short time, but I feel that fate has brought us together. I want you to know I want to marry you. We can get a little apartment at first, and I know with enough hard work we can make a life for ourselves. It will be hard at first. I will not sign up for another tour of duty in the Navy. I'll get a job and work very hard. You can keep your job at RCA. I will buy you a small little house. I will do the outside work and you can do the inside.

I think we can have a wonderful life together. I truly fell in love with you from the first moment I saw you. I love you, all my love now and forever. Your sunny boy, George. February 18, 1948.

The love that blossomed between them was like a gravitational force, pulling them toward each other. Sonny did not sign up for another tour of duty, having met the love of his life. He knew it was time to be a civilian and a husband. He proposed to Loretta, an offer she accepted without hesitation.

On March 17, 1948, Loretta Alexandra Naguszweksi married George William Hlopak at 2:30 in the afternoon at Saint Bridget's Roman Catholic Church in Newark. It was a small ceremony attended by Sonny's mother, Edith, and his sister, Ruth. Loretta's mother and father, and her sister Geraldine were there, with Helen and Gene completing the wedding party.

It was a bright St. Patrick's Day, and while none of them were Irish, they had hoped the luck of the day would rub off on them and bring them happiness—a wish that was soon fulfilled.

After getting a small apartment on Avon Avenue, Sonny quickly landed a job driving a bus for public service. Mother-in-law Sarah used her lifelong skills as a seamstress to make all of the curtains and the tablecloth for their new home.

They worked diligently for their life together. Some days Loretta would hurry off on her lunch break and meet Sonny at one of the stops along his bus route. They would ride the bus for a few stops, then get off and walk home.

When they were able to have lunch together, she would sit beside him and they would talk about their future, sharing dreams they believed could come true if they worked hard enough for them. She would bring him cheese sandwiches she'd made that morning, turning their lunch hour into something magical. And in the evenings they would spend time with Helen and Gene, having quickly become a foursome. Gene was a trained machinist, while Helen worked as a dental technician. Together they started an adventure that for some of them would last a lifetime, from picnics in the warm weather to travel and plans for a future that looked as bright as a noonday sun.

CHAPTER TEN

That's What Friends Are For

1950

Whenever Helen and Gene were spotted on the town, you could be sure Loretta and Sonny were nearby, and usually at the same table. The couples' friendship continued to deepen as the next few years passed. There were dynamics within the foursome as well, with Helen and Loretta bonding as best friends while Gene and George began thinking of business ventures they could do together. As with all close friendships, adjustments had to be made. Among the biggest was Helen and Gene's decision to finally leave the city for something more idyllic and rural. They'd had their fill of trolley cars and bustling crowds. The farming life, or at least a life in the country, called to them from beyond the Newark city limits. They began looking for farm land and soon found just the right property in Watchung, New Jersey, a mere hour's ride by bus or car. It was the perfect solution, allowing them to move into this new phase of their lives without going so far away as to make Newark a distant memory.

Parting was emotional, as it always is between friends, but they knew it wouldn't be long before Loretta and Sonny started making regular trips to visit. It was a pleasant drive, and being on their best friends' land was an adventure. Loretta knew farming from her youth in Nanticoke, and Sonny took to working the land as if he'd grown up with chickens in the yard and vegetables growing just outside the windows.

Helen and Gene set up a vegetable stand to sell their crops and eggs, which also helped them become familiar with their new neighbors. They installed a hatchery for their many chickens, selling the eggs along with their small crops. Loretta cherished her memories of working in the large vegetable garden and learning how to handle all the eggs to make sure they weren't fertilized. She was taught to put them through a lighted device that would reveal any blood spots. If spots were visible, the eggs were known to be fertilized and put back under the chickens to be hatched. It was a fascinating education for them, and she would recall their experiences with great fondness as the years passed.

Gene and Sonny began talking more frequently about land values and the prospect of owning other pieces of property. This was in 1950, when most people worked on farms or in the cities and factories. These two young men decided they would strike out on their own — they just needed to find the right opportunities.

Their business partnership and friendship were well established by then. Gene learned to become a stock broker on the side, and it wasn't long before Sonny took a civil service test to become a police officer in Plainfield, New Jersey, just 25 miles from Newark.

The post-World War II building boom was in full swing, with so many G.I.s returning home and wanting to leave their farms or relocate to an urban setting. The war in Europe had exposed many of them to a bigger world, and they wanted to expand their horizons back in the States. Owning your own home became central to the American dream, with home builders ready and waiting to help them with new construction and even pre-fabricated houses. Assisting in this new boom was the G.I. Bill. Formerly called the Servicemen's Readjustment Act of 1944, the law provided an array of benefits for the returning veterans. (The original G.I. Bill expired in 1956, but the term "G.I. Bill" is still in common use for programs created to assist American military veterans.) The legislation passed through Congress in a bipartisan effort led by the American Legion and included significant benefits, from financial assistance for education to housing and business loans. Many of the returned veterans were able to use this assistance to buy homes, providing there were enough of them for all these prospective homeowners.

The demand for new housing gave birth to what is considered the first suburb, in Levittown, New York, named after the man who perfected affordable housing at the time. The original Levittown house sold for $7,900. The houses were fully furnished with modern appliances, and with help from the G.I. Bill and Federal Housing Subsidies, the up-front cost to the buyers could be as low as $400. A house could be built in a single week, enabling the quick and cost-effective production of similar or identical houses in subdivisions that set the stage for massive and rapid growth across the country. Soon William Levitt had sold 17,000 units, providing homes for 84,000 people. Levitt and his vision for a thriving suburbia made the cover of Time Magazine in July, 1950, with the tagline "For Sale: A New Way of Life."

One of these Levittowns was in Plainfield. The homes were Cape Cod style, consisting of two bedrooms and a dining room, one bath, a tiny kitchen, and an attic. Each lot was 50 ft. X 100 ft., providing just enough room to have a small victory garden and a garage, if the homeowner wanted one.

Some were fortunate enough to afford add-ons they built themselves. It created a uniformity to the subdivisions, with the only difference being the color each family picked for their house.

Remembering the promise he'd made to his young bride Loretta of owning their own home, the Hlopaks bought their first house at 1414 Shirley Street in Plainfield. It was a small piece of heaven, offering new adventures and new friends. It seemed everyone was moving into a brand-new house. Neighbors borrowed sugar from each other, talked across backyard fences, and got together on weekends for barbecues and parties.

One of the families Sonny and Loretta came to know was led by Ted and Carol, a young couple busy growing their nest with babies arriving about every two years. Loretta loved babies, and took particular pleasure in helping Carol with the children as the family expanded. Ted and Carol already had a good start on their brood when Sonny and Loretta moved into the neighborhood. Ted and Carol's first daughter was Linda, born in 1947, followed by Jan in '49, Barb in '50, and Dale in '52. The only glitch for Loretta was that she didn't have any children of her own. Helping out with the kids both was both satisfying and consoling: caring for them was the next best thing to looking after her own. It provided her a vicarious sense of motherhood she longed to have for herself.

As all young couples strive for a better life, Gene became a successful stock broker, while Sonny attended the Police Academy in Plainfield, pursuing his desire to join the Force. Having aced his Naval training years before, he sailed through the Academy with flying colors and loved every minute of it. He was soon an officer on the Plainfield Police Force, and everything was going well for them all.

Just when everyone was getting comfortable and settled in, Gene came home and announced he'd bought the biggest pull-trailer he could find. The 1950s were a golden age for pull-trailers, as the post-World War II boom provided Americans with the prosperity they needed to enjoy their newfound leisure time. Families across the country were embracing the idea of mobility and adventure. Brands like Airstream and Shasta became household names, admired for their sleek designs and innovative features. Airstream, with its iconic silver bullet shape, represented the epitome of mid-century modern design and became synonymous with luxury travel. In 1954 the country got to see the Hollywood celebrities Lucille Ball and Dezi Arnaz travel across the nation in a movie called 'The Big, Big Trailer,' and in no time everyone wanted to hit the open road with a pull-trailer hitched behind their car.

Gene and Helen had been bitten by the pull-trailer bug. It wasn't too big a surprise when they took a great leap of faith, sold their farm, and headed West to California for their next big gamble. The fun wasn't in winning or losing, but in rolling the dice. Once again they said goodbye to Loretta and Sonny, but it wouldn't be for long.

CHAPTER ELEVEN

Here Comes the Sunshine

1951 – 1964

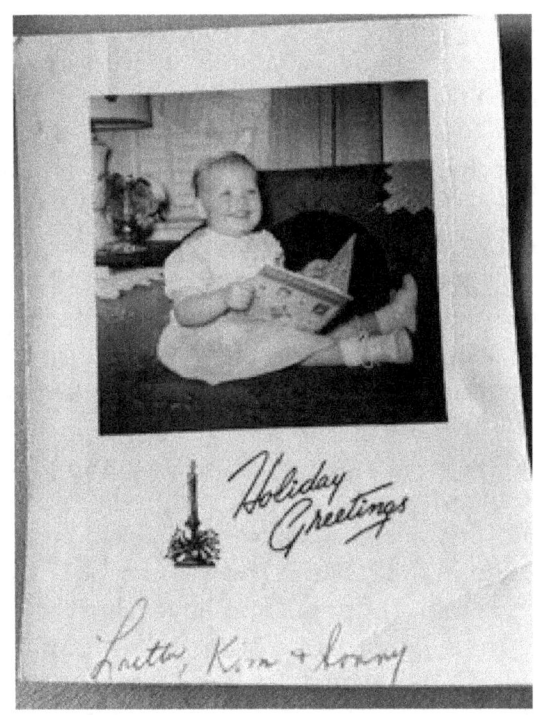

Helen and Gene were busy travelling the country in their trailer, reporting back to Sonny and Loretta on their adventures. It seemed they'd driven to a new destination every week, and Helen would provide detailed reports on their exploits through cards and letters. Back in Plainfield, Sonny and Lorreta were keeping themselves busy focusing on work and following some of Gene's stock advice, growing their small nest egg.

One day Loretta announced to Sonny that their long-held dream of having a child was soon to be a reality, after almost a nine year wait in their marriage to share the joy of parenting.

How we arrive in this world is well known, but the *why* of it remains an inscrutable mystery. Where do we come from? Why are we here? One thing that's not a mystery is that on June 9, 1957, Kim Loretta Hlopak was born. I can't claim to remember anything about that day, but it began the journey I call my life.

Fathers weren't allowed in the delivery room back then. They had to fret in excruciating anticipation, pacing around the waiting room and looking at the wall clock every five minutes. When Sonny was told his daughter had made her dramatic entry onto the world stage, he jumped up and down like a boy who'd gotten his favorite toy for Christmas. He shook every hand in sight and congratulated himself on this momentous occasion. He often said it was the happiest day of his life since he'd met my mother.

My mother tells me a story that it was so hot in June that she carried me on a silk pillow so her arm perspiration wouldn't touch my tiny body. I've never doubted the truth of it, so welcomed was I into this family that now consisted of the three of us. Loretta finally had her baby doll to care for, much like her mother Sarah had years ago. This time the doll would grow into adulthood and have a life of her own.

Now the neighborhood seem to be complete, with Ted and Carol's children playing alongside Loretta's daughter. Their oldest daughter Linda became my best friend, more like a big sister. Linda became an important presence in all of our lives. Both our families were joyful and complete.

None of us children back in the 50s and 60s were put in daycare or watched after by anyone but our mothers and close neighbors. I remember attending picnics, running around with other kids at our neighbors' backyard barbecues, and staying out until dark. We attended church almost every Sunday. My father would pick up Grandma Sarah, who lived in Maplewood by then, or his mother Edith—sometimes both—and off we'd go to Sunday service, followed by a big dinner at home, or to a fancy restaurant. My childhood up to this point was idyllic, with family trips, holidays and birthday parties, something right out of a popular TV show at the time called 'Father Knows Best,' or 'Leave It To Beaver.' I was loved and cherished, and felt it with every fiber of my being.

My father's idea of a day trip could be as far away as a three-hour drive. I laugh when I remember my teenage years and my girlfriends coming home from school with me. Dad would say we were going out for dinner and ask if my friends would like to come along. "Mr. Hlopak wants to know if I can go out to dinner with them," a friend would say, having called her parents for permission. "What state?" they'd ask, only half-joking. We lived in central New Jersey, and dinner out could mean Jersey, Pennsylvania, New York, or even Connecticut. Wherever we went, we'd still be home by late evening and back to school the next day.

These are memories that have stayed with me a lifetime. Some, from an even younger age, are just as indelible. I don't know how early we begin to form lasting memories, but I remember a time when my mother took me to a beautiful house on a lake that had a big picture window facing the water. It was a crisp, cold day. There were a lot of people around. I was a cute small girl with long blonde hair, and everyone seemed to want to touch me, as if I were a prize of some kind. Someone handed me a big doll almost as large as my five-year-old self, and I played with it all afternoon on the ride home. By the time we got back to our house where Dad was waiting for us, I'd fallen asleep. The doll was gone, and when I asked my mother where it went, she insisted there was no doll and I must have been dreaming. It wasn't until years later I discovered it wasn't a dream after all.

***

By the time I'd arrived in the Hlopak household, Gene and Helen had driven their long pull-trailer to a place called Long Beach, California. It was as far west as they could go without driving onto a ship and sailing into the Pacific Ocean.

It also felt like the perfect place to settle down, at least for awhile. The city's waterfront attractions, sprawling coastline, and thriving cultural scene offered the best of several worlds. They fell in love with the whole idea of the West, with its history and its myths, and the climate seemed perfect for any business ventures Gene had in mind.

I was old enough to recognize people, and Helen was a standout. When I was a toddler, my mother had a method of showing me black-and-white photographs of people so I wouldn't be frightened of them when we first met. My earliest recollection of Helen was from our trips to California. She was tall, very thin, with bright red fingernails that were prominent when she smoked a cigarette using a long holder that looked like an extension of her hand. She was glamorous in her own way—not especially pretty, but well put-together. She might be described as a flowing willow tree, with long bleached-blonde hair. It was so light it looked like snow, and she wore it up, held in place with a cloud of hairspray. It reminded me of cotton candy. Between the hairspray and the cigarettes, I'm surprised she never set herself on fire. She had a peculiar laugh and a smoker's cough, and she always smelled of cigarettes. It permeated her clothes and seemed like a permanent odor.

Gene was a smart man who was also kind. He dressed neatly, although not as sharply as my dad. He had an almost Cuban flavor to him. Neither he nor Daddy ever wore blue jeans, always slacks and expensive shoes. Gene was also a chain smoker like Helen, and they would leave a cloud of smoke behind them wherever they went. Gene stood about 5 feet 9 inches, with a full head of hair. He always seemed to be around the ladies and obviously enjoyed their company. He would usually have a scotch on the rocks in hand while they sat on the patio in the cool California evening. And he always read the Wall Street Journal. He had a lot of books around, being an avid reader, and he was very aware of what was going on in the world from day to day. I later discovered I could tell how well the stock market was doing by how much he smoked.

It was the early 1960s, and while my parents felt the same westward pull, my dad had been on the Plainfield, New Jersey, police force for several years and wanted to stay to get his 20-year pension before relocating anywhere. California continued to be a draw, so every year from the time I was nine months old the three of us would travel there. The first time, my mother and I flew while dad drove by himself so we'd have the car for exploring. We were an adventurous trio, two happy parents and one mesmerized child staring out a car window at all the amazing things to see and do.

I was blessed to learn so many things from my grownups: Don't be afraid to try anything, you only have this one life to do it; if you don't know how to do a job, take it on anyway and learn. My father would tell me these things over the years, and they served me well to this day.

I didn't realize back then that I was being prepared for the challenges that come our way in life. I learned to ice skate almost before I could walk. My mother would strap double-bladed skates onto my snow boots and take me to a park in Maplewood, New Jersey. She would bundle me up in my beautiful blue snowsuit, and I'd stumble and fumble on the ice, learning to skate. We seemed to go fairly often. I wasn't more than three years old at the time. I remember, in the gauzy way of our first enduring memories, falling on the ice one time. Within an instant I was picked up from behind by a pair of very strong hands and hoisted up to the sky. They were not my father's hands, and his was not my father's scent. Daddy wore Old Spice, instantly recognizable to generations of children as how their fathers smelled. This man had no hint of aftershave. He put me down and patted me on the head. My mother took my hand and skated us quickly away.

I was taught to ride ponies starting when I was six, the beginning of my love for horses. Along with all the things I learned, travel remained a central passion for the family. Daddy would come home, take off his uniform, lock up his service revolver, and put on his 'Father Knows Best' outfit. He'd switch out his police blues for tailored pants, a nice shirt and, if it was winter, a stylish button-up sweater. Then he would ask my mother where she wanted to go for dinner. She'd never been much of a cook, and it was his way of avoiding her dinners while treating her to an evening out at the same time.

He told us that if we ate in a restaurant three times a week and didn't order steak, we could actually eat out five times. We were well known in all the local restaurants, each one more interesting and colorful than the last, from the waiters to the owners who greeted us as friends. Every time there was a new Radio City Music Hall show we would go into Manhattan to see it. Somehow Sonny always got us front row center seats, and I could lean over the orchestra pit and watch the musicians rise up on the platform as the shows began. Then we would eat at one fine restaurant or another.

During the winters my father would drive to Florida and find somewhere lovely around Miami for us to spend a vacation. There was always a pool for me to swim and splash in while my parents read the daily newspapers. After an afternoon of fun and relaxation, we would head out for a fancy dinner in one of dozens of topnotch restaurants. In the spring we would head to Canada, where I became very familiar with the Canadian side of Niagara Falls. I was always allowed to bring a friend or cousin, providing me with a companion my own age. Summer would come again, and off we'd go on our cross-country trek to California.

If I had kept a written journal of our adventures, it would have taken me pages and pages to describe all the unique locations and people we encountered. The highways were dotted with motels, and my father would drive for six hours or so, pull into one with the must-have swimming pool, and we'd settle in for a night before driving on the next morning.

It wasn't long before I'd driven cross country with them 27 times. Meeting the great variety of people we encountered along the way gave me a deep sense of respect for individuals of all backgrounds and ethnicities. I knew it was a person's heart that mattered, not the color of their skin, or their financial background, and I've never forgotten that.

Our destination on our trips to California was always meeting up with Helen and Gene. It allowed my father and Gene to explore business opportunities. Franchises were just becoming popular then. At one time, Gene and my father owned a Baskin-Robbins franchise, and they'd checked out the very first McDonald's in Santa Barbara. As incredible as it sounds now, you could purchase a McDonald's franchise for $900. In addition to considering these businesses, they bought a mobile home park in Palm Springs, as well as an ice cream and sandwich shop in Lake Tahoe. My father's plan was always to make enough money from his business operations to retire from the Plainfield Police Force and head West, joining Helen and Gene in what was still very much a land of opportunity. Sonny Hlopak was a smart man, and an astute businessman. He knew what he wanted, and he knew the sky was the limit.

What we all learned much too soon was that sometimes the sky really does fall.

CHAPTER TWELVE

Let the Good Times Roll

1959 – 1965

So much has changed in the decades since 1959. It was a world before cell phones and televisions in cars. As hard as it may be to imagine now, people were required to talk to each other. The alternative was to pass the time in silence. The Hlopaks weren't the silent types, so we filled our hours with conversation as we drove from one end of America to the other. My parents would point out scenery and landmarks, and they taught me how to read a map. There was no robot giving us instructions from a GPS. I learned to know the highways, and to adjust to the many detours that were common then. We might come across a herd of cows ambling slowly down a road in Wyoming, or bad weather might force us into seeking shelter when severe storms came our way. I remember a trip through Nevada once when a sandstorm stripped the car of paint. We couldn't wait to get to California where my dad headed off to Tijuana, Mexico, to have the car completely repainted.

Another time we were driving cross-country in a convertible. My mother noticed a small pinhole that had been torn into the top by a hailstorm the day before. By the time we got to California the roof had been sheared and cut in so many places my dad had to stop at a Sears Roebuck and buy a tarp that he attached to the car roof with bungee cords. We looked like the Beverly Hillbillies pulling into Hollywood. The fun these trips provided me helped make me who I am today.

I got to know the country from the back seat of a car. We used maps, and my dad would sit up at night in the motels we stayed at, plotting our next 500 mile drive. Sometimes we would cut it to 300 if there was something interesting to see. I've been almost everywhere because of these experiences, from Niagara Falls, to the Washington Monument, to the Florida Everglades; Mount Rushmore to the Badlands and the Painted Desert, to the Golden Gate Bridge. We even went to Tijuana together to watch a bullfight. He never saw the world as a bad place. As intelligent as he was, he could also be naïve. Not realizing the gore of bullfighting's climax, he took us out of the arena.

One time during Easter season, in the mid-60s, there was growing civil unrest, with racial divisions flaring up across the country. We were driving through Georgia. It was a hot Easter Sunday. Daddy never missed going to church on Sundays, and when he saw one we pulled into the parking lot. The windows were wide open — air conditioning was a luxury many people couldn't afford — and we heard the sweet sound of singing pour out into the air. Holding hands, the three of us entered and realized we were the only white people there. The ladies in the pews wore big, bright Easter hats, and the congregation sang as one with their amazing voices. My father reminded us that skin color was no barrier between us. They were singing and praising Jesus, and we fit right in. I've never forgotten the pleasant smell of sweat mixed with perfume, the big gorgeous hats, and the memories they gave me. Everything felt as if the world was exactly the way it should be, but things were about to change.

***

In 1963, the nation was rocked by the assassination of John F. Kennedy, America's youngest President. The country went into mourning, and for the next few years tensions grew increasingly inflamed. There were over 150 riots in the summer of 1967, stretching from Los Angeles to Newark. The riots even reached Plainfield, where my dad was still a police officer. The violence there lasted from June 14 through 16. Rocks were thrown, shootouts occurred. There was arson and looting all through the town. It was rumored that people had been recruited from out of the area to create chaos and fear.

Daddy always left his work at the door when he came home. He would change his clothes, leave his work responsibilities in the closet with his uniform, and become my dad. The burdens of being a police officer were never shared with us.

I was sheltered in many ways for so much of my young life. This was the era of political assassinations and violence, claiming the lives of Martin Luther King, Jr., President Kennedy, and his brother Bobby. My parents did a good job of explaining the nature of evil and how it manifested in so many ways, irrespective of or race or income, but I was protected from those realities to a degree. My father's handling of very adult experiences that a child can have difficulty understanding increased my love for him beyond belief. Daddy was always my hero.

No one knew what would happen next, but it seemed danger was all around us. During the Plainfield riots, George Hlopak, police officer, performed his duty as expected. He would never have done less. He was struck by a car and injured on the same day another officer was killed. It was a terrifying time. I remember being driven to school in the back of his police cruiser with a blanket over me.

The events of that summer would shape the rest of our lives. My father's injury had lasting implications for his health and for his family. We had no way of knowing it then, but that car had crashed into all of us.

CHAPTER THIRTEEN

Church and Changes

1967

Church had always been an important part of our family life. Nearly every Sunday we would head to my grandmother Edith and Aunt Ruth's church, where they had a fantastic organ that seemed almost magical to me. The organist would play songs while her fingers glided over the keys and her feet danced on the pedals. Music would fill the sanctuary, and I would sit in a pew staring up at the magnificent stained glass windows. Every color imaginable was there in intricate designs that portrayed images from the Bible. One was a portrait of Jesus holding a lamb and walking forward, surrounded by bright, beautiful colors refracting the outside light through their carefully cut pieces. I remember attending services and being enthralled by it all, with the images of the windows embedding themselves in my young memory so deeply I've never forgotten them.

After the service we would head to my grandmother Sarah's church, which was different in so many ways. She'd been raised and remained Catholic her entire life. The customs and rituals there were very different, with parishioners putting our hands in water when we first entered the church, and kneeling for a few seconds on padded boards behind the pews. Sarah had a string of beads, which I later learned were for the Catholic tradition of saying the Rosary. She would count them with her fingers, and I would watch her lips move as she spoke silently and moved the beads in her hand. I remember the smell of scented candles, with a wonderful aroma that can still take me back to those times when I encounter it. All my cousins from that side of the family seemed much more familiar with the traditions and expectations than I was.

When my parents married, my father never criticized my mother for any of her beliefs. The unconditional love he showed her, and the way he explained the God he served, made so much sense to me. He made it real and personal. He used to say to love the sinner, hate the sin. Look into that person's heart that may have been hardened by their circumstances. They just needed the love and understanding God offers them. It was this mixture of love and belief that I would carry with me when I began spending a lot of time at Terrill Road Bible Chapel in Fanwood, New Jersey. Begun as a small meeting in 1870 in Plainfield, it became a church body in 1931 and moved to Fanwood in 1957. For over 100 years, Terrill Road has continued to serve the community, and it was a vital part of my own faith journey.

I remember seeing puppet shows that described the gospel. I can still recite the song, "Jesus loves me this I know, for the Bible tells me so." There was a lyric in the song about a little Indian boy "with a bow and arrow for his toy." Using puppets to act out the song made a lasting impression on my child's mind. I knew there had to be meaning behind all this, but I wasn't always sure what it was.

Linda remained a great influence on my life. I called her my sister even though we weren't related. Linda had big, beautiful blue eyes and long blonde hair that flowed down to the middle of her back. Her smile was ear-to-ear, and she had an infectious laugh that just made you want to be around her more. She never wore makeup or painted her fingernails. A woman of many talents, she taught me how to ski and drive. There wasn't much she couldn't do, and she took care of me as if were in the same family. She would often take me to church herself. If Daddy was around he and my mother would come, but if he was on a business trip my mother would drop me off and not come into the church. Little did I realize back then she was acting from the trauma and the Catholic guilt of her upbringing she had from things in her past. It was the summer of my 10th year when I longed for my mother to become part of our church family. My girlfriends' mothers were all volunteering to work at vacation Bible school, and I thought it would be wonderful if Mom would join us. I would feel so proud. So I made the bold move one Sunday of volunteering my mother to work there. When I got home and made the announcement, she became angry with me. I wasn't sure why—it seemed like such a good opportunity for mother and daughter—but Daddy wasn't around and she would sometimes change when he wasn't present.

Mother used to become more nervous when my father wasn't there to keep her calm. It was around that time, when I turned 10, that I really started to pay attention to the differences in her mood and personality. If Sonny wasn't home, she would treat me in ways that felt cold and distant. I knew she loved me, but something had started to feel off about it all. I'd told her we'd just been taught the story of Jonah. I asked her if she could imagine a man being swallowed by a whale and spit out after he'd obeyed God, landing safely on the beach. She looked at me as if she had no idea what I was talking about, as I continued describing the craft we would be making. "All you have to do is help," I said. The kids had put sand on cardboard to make it look like the beach where Jonah landed after being expelled from the whale. We were going to paint the water, and the men who volunteered there would make tiny boats we would glue onto it. I assumed she would find it as fantastic as I did, but she was completely disinterested. Bible school was scheduled for two weeks, and my mother showed up for four days. I made excuses to the others, saying she had a headache. I didn't understand why she'd reacted that way. The other ladies were all prim, proper and kind, and Mom was so beautiful. I didn't understand why she felt like she wouldn't fit in.

It wouldn't be until years later that I started to see a real picture of what was going on, but it was that same time in the summer of 1967 that Mr. Smart, a traveling pastor, made a chalk drawing to illustrate a point about the biblical verse, John 3:16, which states, *"For God so loved the world that he gave his one and only Son, that whoever believes in him shall not perish but have eternal life." The drawing was beautiful, but when he turned off the lights and switched on a blacklight, a different picture emerged from the drawing.* He explained how salvation means God wants to be your forever friend. When you believe in Jesus, you're never alone, and God promises to always love you and be with you, here on earth and in heaven.

Jesus loves us as we are, no matter what we've done. This was the beginning of my understanding that there's a God who takes care of me. In my child's mind I felt something different happening that summer. When I heard that man's talk and saw his demonstration, it felt like I was floating on a cloud. He told us that God isn't waiting for us to mess up, and He's not angry with us. We don't need to be afraid – his love is a gift, not a test.

I got home and told Daddy right away and he knew what I'd experienced. He put his arms around me and told me I was now a daughter of the King. I didn't understand what he meant, but our connection became stronger than when he'd been just my Dad. I shared this with Mom and she was slightly dismissive of it. It would be years before the pieces of this puzzle, as well as the puzzle of my mother, came together in the mosaic of my life.

It was a wonderful summer that year. Linda was 10 years older than I was and could drive by then. It allowed me to be a sidekick on lots of adventures. It was also a challenging time, since Linda had already left for college and we only had the summers to spend together. She taught me so many things when she was able to. She taught me to paint; she took me to Girl Scouts; and she introduced me to Terrill Road Bible Chapel. If Linda said something was true, I believed her. She was the most kind, loving person I'd met besides my father. Linda was instrumental in teaching me about God, and how He was creating this tapestry of my life even without me knowing it.

As a ten year old, these were among the biggest changes of my life. I was no longer a child to be played with and coddled as if I were still a baby. I had a mind of my own, and a growing awareness of the world I lived in—especially of the adults, and more specifically my mother. I believed she'd begun to see me as competition for my father's attention. I could tell from her moods and words that she didn't like it. Thank goodness for Linda, who would often show up at our house just when my mother was about to spin slightly out of control. Linda had a way of calming her down, just like my father did.

I remember my mother telling me that I was not allowed to hug Daddy like I used to, that I was becoming too big of a girl and that I shouldn't do that anymore. It put a pain on my heart because my father was everything to me. We were sitting in the kitchen one afternoon with my grandmother Sarah, and she asked my mother, "Did you give Kim a permanent?" I had straight blonde hair, and suddenly it became curly with adolescence. Mom abruptly got up from the table, fetched a hair iron and started to straighten my hair with more force than she needed. It hurt, and I looked at her with questioning eyes, *Why are you doing this to me?* Grandmother even told her to stop.

My grandmother Sarah Rose was just 4 feet 11 inches tall, and I had adored her as a child. I would sit in her lap and laugh at whatever had struck me as funny. She would say her rosary all the time, running her fingers along the beads. She was a kind woman who I'd never seen be mean to anyone. She wore glasses and she was always nicely but simply dressed. As she got older she started wearing pantsuits, completely different from Grandma Edith. Sarah made you feel as if you could confide in her, and I did. I remember her drinking a beer with an egg cracked into it, which I never understood. She was 100 percent Polish and spoke both Polish and fluent English. She cooked all the Polish dishes, passing her culture on to the next generation. I adored her, and she would always tell me to be good to my mother. It was as admonition that had become harder for me to stick to with my mother's volatility.

It seemed the family I'd seen as perfect was changing. I didn't like it or understand it. Then Dad came home one afternoon and announced we were moving. Mother and I would head to California to live with Helen and Gene until Daddy retired from the police force, then he would join us for a new life in the Golden State. He promised to build us a beautiful house, and I began to imagine its rooms and its wonderful spaces.

I had no way of knowing my world was about to crash headlong into the unexpected. I didn't understand how such a wonderful reality could change so quickly, and without warning.

CHAPTER FOURTEEN

The Golden State

1968

Time passed as quickly as youth. It seemed to last just moments—an idyllic childhood where mom and dad were the center of my universe; where Linda, my cousins, and all my wonderful friends were part of my everyday life. I had my first crush on a neighbor boy named David. I remember laughing together in the snow, rolling down the lawn and making angels whose wings would melt away all too soon, leaving only outlines in the cold grass beneath.

I attended private schools. My parents were were well known in the community. Family church routines were similar, and everything felt perfect to me. I was even Dorothy in my school's production of *The Wizard of Oz*. As if all that weren't enough, I was the head Girl Scout cookie seller, making my mother so very proud of me. She showed me off like a little doll wherever we went. I felt special around her, being introduced as her princess. My parents seemed happy to me, but when my mother and I were sent to California ahead of my father, it felt as if it were all slipping away as surely as those snow angels had vanished.

The trip this time was different. Daddy was in a hurry to get us out West where we would live with Helen and Gene while we waited to be reunited in a home of our own. He would come out to visit every few months as promised, using the time for he and Gene to explore business opportunities. I was trying to make sense of it all in my young girl way, confused but fascinated by the sudden changes. Mom and Dad would sit in the front seat when we rode in the car. She would put her hand on his neck and stroke it tenderly. He would hold her hand while he drove. But I remember this time it felt different. It was quieter. There wasn't as much music playing on Daddy's eight-track, his tapes of Frank Sinatra pouring out their soothing sounds less frequently. I didn't understand what was happening, only that *something* was off. My father's mood had changed, but I was certain once we got to the Golden Coast, as Daddy called it, everything would be normal and happy again.

I never saw my father angry, but he and my mother were strangely silent on that trip. We got to Long Beach ahead of schedule. My mother and I settled into Helen and Gene's guest room, while Daddy only stayed one night before heading on the long drive back to New Jersey. He promised he'd be back soon, and that sometimes he would fly out instead to hasten his return. He didn't like flying, preferring the wide open feeling of a car. Mom and I shared a bedroom, which was also something that felt odd to me. I didn't like the bed. It was uncomfortable and unfamiliar, but Helen and Gene had always been like an aunt and uncle to me so I couldn't say anything. They made me feel welcome, offsetting the sense I had that something wasn't quite right.

We had grapefruit and avocado trees in the yard. There was a lovely patio with an awning to sit under in the sun. I spent many quiet hours there painting, reading, and growing up. I was enrolled in school, and I liked it there. It was so different from the schools back East. The classrooms were all square, with open-air hallways. I could walk outside to my next class, and the lunch room was more like a large pavilion that would fill up with students, the sounds of our lunch trays and chatter permeating the room. I could eat outside on picnic tables when the weather was good, which it almost always was. I learned new playground games, and played hopscotch and jump rope. I was also able to make a few new girlfriends.

There was one boy, named Ellis, who everyone seemed to pick on. He didn't quite fit in with the other kids, and his clothes looked as if they'd been handed down from an older sibling. They were different from the types of clothing most of us wore. He was quiet and shy, and he always ate alone. He sometimes wore overalls to school, and his hands and fingernails were dirty, as if he'd been working on a farm. But he was always nice to me. One day he asked if he could walk me home, and I was surprised and happy to have his company. We talked a little, and it gave me the comforting feeling of being watched over. He was kind and polite, and I knew he went from there to his own home that would be very different from mine.

I was still young and in need of adult supervision, so it was decided I should have a nanny. I don't know how old Mrs. Deerson was, but to me she seemed about 90. She lived across the street from Helen and Gene's house, and I would walk home to her. She'd ask me to do my studies at her dining room table. If I finished them and was well-behaved, she'd let me go swimming in her built-in pool. It wasn't as fun as it could have been because she watched every stroke I took. I didn't know how strong a swimmer I was until then. I was used to my parents letting me just splash and play, but Mrs. Deerson kept close watch on me. It was uncomfortable, and I never stayed in the pool very long.

Mrs. Deerson would recount stories from her childhood. She'd come across the Rio Grande from Mexico by horseback to live with her nephew in California. She married Mr. Deerson and they remained together but childless for 40 years — apparently they were unable to have children. She was stricter than most of the adults I knew, but also a very sweet woman. She would undo my braids and brush my hair 100 times, telling me it was good for the roots and would make my hair grow longer. If I was really good, she would make her homemade fudge and teach me while she did it.

I also learned to ride a skateboard. I would glide up and down the neighborhood having great fun, but I missed my dad terribly. He would call almost every night. It was expensive then, when long distance calls were a separate charge. It was years before cell phones, answering machines and caller ID. You never knew who was going to be on the other end of the line when you answered. One afternoon in particular I was back at Helen and Gene's house, and no one was home yet. The phone rang, and when I answered it I heard the polite voice of a man with a sense of humor I detected in his tone even then.

"Hello, Doll, how are you?" he said.

"Who is this?" I replied.

He wouldn't tell me who he was. He simply said, "Tell your mom we're watching over her, and if she needs us she knows how to find me. You're looking good, kid."

Then he hung up, just like that. When my mother came home we were the only two there, and I told her about the phone call from the strange man. She was dismissive at first, but when I walked past the phone she grabbed the receiver, and for the first time my mother struck me. She hit me so hard in the shoulder that I cried out of shock. I'd never been physically disciplined, and I'd always been on my best behavior. I was truly a good kid, and the experience was extremely confusing to me.

My mother could simply give me a stern look and I would stop in my tracks. This was the first time she'd actually hit me with an object, telling me to go to my room. I couldn't understand what was happening, or why, and I grabbed our dog and ran into my bedroom. I cried into my pillow so she wouldn't hear me. To make it all even more disorienting, she later told me never to mention this to my father. I sensed I would be hit again if I did.

I hadn't yet learned to bury my feelings, and certainly not to hate her for it at that age. Instead, I withdrew deep into myself, yearning for my father to come back. I wanted to rush to the airport and see him walking toward me. I didn't care if it meant waiting hours for the plane to arrive. I just wanted Daddy to get there, and Mom to kiss him on the cheek. He would hold her hand for a moment before she pulled it away. I would run and jump into his arms and get a huge bear hug. I would feel safe with him around, and we would resume our adventures.

When he did get back, he told my mother he had several business meetings lined up. She, Helen and Gene were to accompany him, and I was allowed to go along. These were some of the best times of my life. I'd been trained to sit quietly while they had their adult conversations. We had no PlayStations or smartphones, or anything to occupy my young mind. Instead, I observed everything around me, listening to them talk about business. One opportunity was at Baskin-Robbins in Burbank. It was my favorite meeting to be at because of the ice cream lab downstairs. They made different ice creams, and I was allowed to visit with some of the workers and taste their flavors all day.

Another time we drove to Lake Tahoe. There was a second ice cream parlor Dad and Gene were interested in buying. This one was in a stone building on a corner — location was always important — and when you sat on its porch you could see part of the lake. It provided a gorgeous view we enjoyed while my parents sat and talked it all over. They discussed making a deal for the ice cream parlor while I was allowed to go around and ask people if they would like some water. I was given the position of water girl, pouring water and talking to potential customers. One man even gave me a quarter tip for my efforts. It was a great experience, and my parents had started to laugh again, a welcome sound I'd been missing.

Daddy was excited with his two new business ventures, but time passed quickly and he soon left for Plainfield while Mom and I stayed behind. I cried for days, but life went on whether I was upset or not. Mom, Helen, Gene and I ate out nearly every night, since neither of the women liked to cook.

We would find new restaurants and revisit ones we enjoyed. I knew where we'd eat according the day of the week. If it was Wednesday, we'd dine at Sal's little Italian restaurant with the red-and-white checked tablecloths. A candle stuck into the neck of an old wine bottle was set in the middle of each table, and the melting wax flowed down in a rainbow of layered colors. Sal was a nice man, as I remember him. He would pinch my cheek, which children tend to find annoying, but he meant well, and his garlic bread was terrific.

We met an Italian couple whose English was poor but passable, and we would all sit underneath the restaurant's arbor and have the best lasagna. A man named Lou would take out his accordion and play in the evenings. It all made for a memorable childhood, but there wasn't a lot there for me to enjoy as a young girl.

Gene had become a successful stock broker, and we could gauge how well the stock market was doing by his cigarette habit. If the market was rough, he'd inhale three packs a day. If the market was doing well, he'd drop it to a half pack. Some days I was allowed to visit his office with him and sit quietly watching the ticker tape go by. Back them before computers were in use, it was fascinating to see all these people stare at the tape with their pens and notepads, then run back and forth to the brokers. A stock market ticker tape was like a long message strip that told what was happening with a stock. A moving line of letters and numbers each had a short "nickname" identifying the stock. The tape was recording transactions on the New York Stock Exchange. Ticker tape was used in 1929 when the stock market crashed, and well into the 1960s.

The office reeked of smoke, which I hated, and by lunch time I invariably had a headache from the smell. If the market was doing well I'd ask Gene to take me out for lunch just to get away from the toxic air. If it wasn't good, I had to wait until the closing bell rang because it was three hours earlier in California.

We left early sometimes and Mom would go off with Gene to meet clients. I would stay with Helen, who was working as a dental technician. She loved her career. She got to make false teeth and work with clay impressions. She also had a fondness for drinking, and would sometimes say jokingly that she was a 'raging alcoholic.' I'd never been around that much drinking. No one in my family in New Jersey really drank. There were days I'd come home and see a vodka bottle on the counter. Helen would be asleep on the couch. She'd have been smoking all day, and the house would stink of cigarettes. I would retreat to the patio outside, or to Mrs. Deerson's house. I couldn't tolerate the odor, and I would ask if Daddy was coming home.

My father had promised to build us a house and start a new life, and it seemed to be taking forever. In the meantime, Mom and Gene would take me to business meetings with them. One occasion stood out and was quite interesting. Gene and Dad had purchased rental cottages on a piece of property. All of the units' backyards faced into a single middle area. There were aspiring actors living there, and some who'd reportedly had their dreams of success come true. One man was said to be very famous and had rented the bungalow as a getaway from the stresses of fame and fortune. He had a big house somewhere else, but he enjoyed coming to the cottage sometimes, and he allowed his housekeeper to stay there. He had a pet squirrel monkey that was kept outside, leashed to a long clothesline that let him roam with limited freedom. One afternoon I was given some apples and allowed to feed him, providing me with a break from the general boredom. The monkey jumped on my shoulder and I screamed. There was a small amount of blood from where the monkey bit me, and my mother came out to see what the commotion was. I found out later the famous actor was Rock Hudson. Having learned more about him years later, it was not surprising he'd value his privacy.

When my father was back he would take me to the Farmer's Market in Los Angeles. A lot of famous people could be seen there, from actors and writers, to successful musicians of the day. It wasn't uncommon for me to find myself sitting at a table next to one celebrity or another. I didn't know who they were, but everyone else seemed to recognize them.

I remember a baker there, long before bakers and cooks became TV personalities. He had a large glass window facing into his bakery, and you could stand and watch him decorate cakes. Sometimes he would put a champagne bottle in the center of a cake and make pink elephants on the sides with frosting. It was all very fascinating. There was also a myna bird at the front of a pet store, and when you walked by it would say hello. Another time we drove up to Seal Beach and ate at a restaurant with a view of seals on the rocks just beyond the shore. Other times we drove to San Francisco and rode the trolleys. It was all amazing to me, made perfect by my father's presence.

That particular summer the five of us drove to Palm Desert. Dad and Gene bought a mobile home park. Mom was to manage the property and we would settle there, waiting patiently for Dad to finish his time with the Plainfield Police, get his pension and join us in our own version of paradise. Once that had been accomplished, he would build us a house near Lake Tahoe. That was the dream, and it was all coming together — so we thought — but sometimes you wake up from a dream just to see it fade away.

CHAPTER FIFTEEN

Too Much for Young Eyes

1969

I loved that little village near Lake Tahoe. The largest alpine lake in North America, Lake Tahoe straddles the border of California and Nevada high in the Sierra Nevada mountains. The area experienced a migration boom in the 1800s with the discovery of silver in the nearby Comstock Lode, leading to a rapid settlement and deforestation of the land for timber. In the 20th century Lake Tahoe evolved into a prime destination for recreation and tourism, appreciated for its visual clarity, wide variety of outdoor activities, and as a setting for high-end retreats and winter sports. While not everyone has been there, it's a safe bet almost everyone has heard of it. It's like Hollywood or Niagara Falls that way — its reputation precedes it.

The views were stunning. You could see the water from almost every vantage point. One time when we drove there, Daddy pulled over and stopped. I remember huge Ponderosa pines climbing up to the sky. The smell of them was so distinct and memorable, permeating the air. They smelled like Christmas, evoking everything about that magical holiday with just their scent. Daddy told me this was where our new home would be — he'd recently bought the lot our home would be constructed on. I was so excited we were finally going to be together again. California was such a unique environment, with all four seasons rolled into one unforgettable moment after another at the lake.

Springtime is beautiful there, yet you can still have massive snow storms arriving almost without warning. You can go skiing in the morning, then drive for a few hours and be in Los Angeles by mid-afternoon. A few hours later you can find yourself in the hot desert, the air and sand cooling off as the sun goes down.

We drove back to the mobile home park now owned my parents with Helen and Gene. I'd hoped that Daddy's announcement of buying a building lot where he and Mom would construct our new home sooner than expected would bring happiness to my mother, but she continued to seem distant. She was a beautiful woman who turned heads in any room she entered, with all eyes glancing around to see her — including the other women, who didn't always appreciate the attention she naturally drew to herself. The men appraised her with obvious approval, but that was the kind of presence she had. She was always well-dressed, and she knew how to work a room, as they say. Yet something had changed in our family dynamics. I thought maybe it was because Daddy was living on the East Coast and we were on the opposite side of the continent. I hoped and prayed that once we were all together in our new house this fraying fabric would stitch itself back together again. I missed Linda, and my grandmother and my cousins, but I would have given anything just to have our small family together and whole. I made myself be satisfied trying to make the days last before Daddy headed back to New Jersey. That inevitable separation came, and I found myself once again in a state of longing.

I went back to school with a head full of dreams for the wonderful life I believed was coming someday. Daddy had promised it, and he always kept his promises. Meanwhile, Gene was off every workday to his stock market job, and Helen returned to drinking, her favorite pastime by then. One day I wasn't feeling well and left school—you didn't need a parental permission slip in those days. My trusted friend Ellis offered to walk me home to make sure I arrived safely. The school allowed us both to leave for the half-hour walk home. We talked about our hopes and dreams the way kids do. When I got home I took out my key, knowing I wasn't going to Mrs. Deerson's house. Mom, Helen, Gene and I were all supposed to go out to dinner that night. I waved goodbye to Ellis and slipped my key into the door. To my surprise, the lock opened but the door did not. The chain had been put across it, something that only happened at night as an added security measure, and often not even then. I could see inside, and my eyes fell on the gold embroidered couch. I will never get the memory of that couch out of my mind. There was my mother, fully clothed, lying together with Gene. Sandwiched, one on top of the other, and kissing. I froze at the sight, and moments later the door was slammed shut and the chain drawn back. When the door opened again, Gene was straightening his hair and saying, "Hey, Kiddo, you're home early." As if they had not been doing what I'd just seen with my own eyes.

I walked straight to my room and never spoke of what I'd witnessed. How could I make sense of my mother kissing another man? The image was burned into my heart, making it cold against her. How dare she betray my father like that? I shut my bedroom door and didn't come out that whole evening, even when they called me to go with them to dinner. It was the first time I stayed home by myself, and it became something I never told anyone, including the man who would be most hurt by it: my beloved father.

It seemed like an eternity before Daddy came back to California. While I'd waited for him, counting the days and nights, I had moped around the house, making a sad presence of myself. When he finally arrived, it was as if the sun had broken through the clouds.

"Let's walk down to the pier," he'd say, or, "Let's go to the beach."

He could sense something was wrong, but I wouldn't dream of telling him what I'd seen, and I never did.

"Do you want to go to the mountains?" he said. "What's the matter, Sunshine?"

It was a terrible balancing act, keeping this awful secret while I tried to hide my feelings as best I could. I was just a child. It's not easy for children to conceal their feelings so completely. I felt as if my world was caving in. I knew how wrong my mother's actions had been, yet I dared not say a word.

We all drove out to the desert to see the mobile home park. I burst into tears, unable and unwilling to say what my emotions were about. I was sure my mother was terrified I would let that screeching cat out of the bag, but I kept her secret. I didn't speak about it to him, and she and I never broached the subject. It was a poisonous seed that had been planted, and that grew for a very long time.

After everything that had happened, and what I'd *seen*, I began to beg Daddy to take us back to New Jersey. "Please," I pleaded, "can we just go back to New Jersey? I hate California. We have to go home, please." Little did I know that within a few short weeks we would be on a plane returning to New Jersey. I was overwhelmed with relief to get out of the situation I'd been in. But more shocks were just around the corner. When we got back, I discovered our beautiful home had been sold and my father was buying a house I disliked the rest of my life there. He'd had to invest quickly for tax purposes, and he only had a few years remaining on the police force. After that we were supposed to move back to California and build our dream house in Lake Tahoe.

I couldn't have imagined that house would become a kind of coffin for my father, and in some ways for me, too. I hated the house, and I believed I'd started to hate my mother. I longed for the life we'd all had so recently, before we moved to California.

CHAPTER SIXTEEN

Home Not Sweet Home

1970

One day Daddy came home to announce he'd bought a motorhome. It was intended to provide us with a sense of adventure when we drove between New Jersey and California, and other places of interest. He thought we should do a small trip so we drove to Florida. I recall us driving across the Chesapeake Bay Bridge-Tunnel in Virginia while Mother and I ate breakfast on the small table looking out the window of the window. The Bridge-Tunnel, considered one of the engineering wonders of the modern world, links Virginia's Eastern Shore to Virginia Beach and the mainland United States. Approximately 17.6 miles long, it's a combination of bridges and tunnels crossing the mouth of the Chesapeake Bay. Completed in 1964, it's system is composed of low-level trestles, high bridges, artificial islands, and two mile-long underwater tunnels that are as amazing to look as they are to travel across.

When we arrived in Florida, we stayed in the motorhome so Mother could visit her family there. After several days we continued on our journey. At one point Mother refused to sleep in the motorhome so my father, being a gentleman and a husband who did his best to placate her, pulled into a lovely hotel. He slept in the motorhome, while she and I checked into a room. I was able to swim again in the hotel pool, which was always comforting to me and a welcome distraction from all the emotions I had swirling around.

Daddy parked and made it a sort of sanctuary for himself. He would go out there on a Sunday and read the newspaper, drink a cup of coffee, and write notes while he read his Bible. He read the scriptures a lot, even when we were on our family trips. Yet I could tell the spark had gone out of him. He and Mother were polite to each other, but the tenderness I'd observed so often between them was gone. One day when he and I took a ride into town, he said to me while driving, "Why doesn't she love me anymore?" It was a rare time that I saw him cry. I felt like screaming inside and telling him she didn't love me anymore either. It was very confusing, and I wondered what was going on. This was my family. It felt as if we were falling apart, but I had no explanation. Daddy was a man of God who loved us and took care of us. He was my knight in shining armor, and she was tarnishing that armor.

The new feeling of anger towards my mother was like a silent bomb waiting to go off on her. It was a blessing to have Linda around, who always seemed to show up for me when I needed it most. I could throw my arms around her, hug her for comfort, and head off on some simple adventure to take my mind off everything that was occupying my thoughts. I didn't tell Linda what was happening, fearful that if I did it would make all the things I was worried about even more real than they were. I was growing up now, and Linda was going to teach me to drive, giving me lessons in a local parking lot. Our bond had only grown since I was little. We went skiing together in the winter, to the beach in the summer, and to church. One of my favorite summer destinations was Island State Beach Park. One of New Jersey's last significant remnants of a barrier island ecosystem that once existed along much of the Atlantic coast, it remains an undeveloped barrier beach. With over 3,000 acres and 10 miles of coastal dunes, it's been untouched since Henry Hudson first described New Jersey's coast from his ship, the Half Moon, in 1609.

Linda and I became inseparable, and I could not have been more thankful for her. In some ways it saved me from losing myself among all my fears and worries.

Daddy soon bought Mother and I a second house, this one in Pennsylvania. It was near a creek, and she and I would spend weekends and holidays there, as well as the summer. He only had two years to go until he could retire from the Plainfield police, then we would all move back to California. That was the plan. He'd be free to build our dream house. In the meantime, Gene flew back a lot to see Daddy and talk about business. Our subsequent trips out West had been reduced to once or twice a year to see their properties. Gene was very polite to my father and from all appearances they were still best friends. Daddy had no idea what Gene was doing with Mother. I didn't fault Gene at the time. My mother was beautiful, and Helen was an active alcoholic. They had no children, and Gene always remained a nice man to me. But I knew what they both were doing to our family.

I didn't know many of the other kids well because I hadn't really grown up with them. This was a new school, and as much as I liked it, the only thing of real value I got from it was my best friend at the time, Susan. Her family attended our church, and they were wonderful to me. Sue and I rode our bikes all through the township of North Plainfield. Sue and a few girlfriends would be asked to go on some adventure with us — Mother was still not a great cook.

Then one night when I was sleeping I felt a fist against my chest. I woke up, dazed from sleep, wondering what was going on. I was dragged out of bed, and my mother beat me badly.

She was always careful not to leave bruises. My father had made a trip back to California, leaving me alone with her, feeling as if there was no one to protect me. The next day I woke up and she acted as if nothing had happened. I couldn't make sense of any of it. It was impossible for me to understand why she was doing that to me. I rode my bike to Susan's house, one of the few places I felt safe, but I never told my friend what was going on. I sat with her in silence, unable to speak about it. It wouldn't be the last time my mother hit me during those difficult months, and I knew if I'd said anything about it to anyone it would make things worse. Who would believe me? Children aren't always believed about this kind of abuse, and back then it was even less likely. I sank into such despair that I thought my life would be better off if I ended it. I was the golden child, after all. I didn't sneak drinks like some of the kids, I didn't run around with boys. I went to church. Yet I was convinced this woman, this *mother*, who professed to love me actually hated me. I wouldn't know the reasons for that until many years later, but that house was suffocating me and I hated living there.

Everything I'd once turned to for a sense of security had vanished. We were back in New Jersey, where I'd wanted desperately to return after feeling lost and unhappy those last months in California, yet so much had changed. I didn't recognize the world I'd found myself in. Even my paternal grandmother and my aunt were different—older, less inclined to treat me as the child I wasn't anymore. They used to have Sunday dinners with us, but that routine had changed.

Growing up was proving difficult and taking a terrible toll, because it wasn't what growing up was supposed to be like. I wasn't supposed to be hit by my mother, or called a liar. I wasn't supposed to feel abandoned by the people I trusted to take care of me and look out for me. But there I was, feeling all those things, with the exception of a loving God who had not, and never would turn His back on me.

I honestly wondered sometimes if I was losing my mind. My mother would accuse me of lying when I told her what I was experiencing. One time I'd made a new friend, whose name I don't recall, and we were at her house enjoying their swimming pool. Our mothers were having coffee and talking. Mom told me to get out of the pool, and when we got home she said I would not be friends with that girl anymore. I was shocked and surprised—why would I not be friends with someone who'd just come into my life? The girl came to me later and confirmed that we were not to be friends. She said our mothers had spoken about it, and Mom had told her mother I was a liar. She'd said I made up stories, and it cut me to the heart. What stories was she talking about? Why would she try to alienate me from other people, let alone a possible new companion? I never understood why she said these things, but it cost me a friend I could have relied on in a world that was getting more and more confusing.

I never talked or went to the girl's house again. My grandmother and aunt pulled further away from us without any explanation to me. Daddy would go and visit them with me and Mother, while at the same time he began to physically change. He seemed ill—you could see it in his face. No one knew what might be happening. He was often in pain, and to Mother's credit, she stepped up and helped him as best she could. She began doting on him again. I had no way of knowing how serious it was or would become, only that my beloved father was in great discomfort and we couldn't make it go away.

CHAPTER SEVENTEEN

The Long Summer

1976

I met a boy named Carl who soon became my first boyfriend and who, unsurprisingly, was a lot like my father. He was tall and handsome, and the kind of upstanding young man Daddy approved of. He didn't swear or misbehave. He knew my father, and they seemed to like each other. He even went to church—a big plus for us. He and his family were well-known in town, and it felt like a good fit. He was kind and considerate. He appeared to really care about me, and he was adventurous like my father.

Daddy started to have backaches that grew increasingly painful, so he made an appointment with a chiropractor. The back adjustments he got from the doctor seemed to help for awhile, but he had also started losing weight. I was getting closer to my high school graduation, and I was distracted by the excitement of it.

That last summer in Plainfield my parents went off to the shore for a couple days. Our lives appeared to be returning to normal, and Carl and I were happy teenagers in love. We soon began going on day trips together just like Mom and Dad used to do. We played music on the car radio, listening to the top songs of the day, everything from Glen Campbell's *Rhinestone Cowboy* to Elton John's *Philadelphia Freedom*. I would hold his hand, and sometimes rub his neck the way my mother did with my father. The world seemed to have righted itself. For a short time I was happy again, and I knew God was with me. He had not abandoned me during my darkest days, and I knew He never would.

One afternoon I got home and Daddy wasn't there. I was told he was in the hospital. I couldn't understand any of it—he'd been healthy, except for the back pain we attributed to his being hit by the car during the Plainfield riots. Carl picked me up and we went to see Daddy, and I was told on the way that he had advanced cancer. It was as if a boulder had fallen out of the sky and landed directly on me. In the morning everything had been wonderful, but by the afternoon it had all come tumbling down. I screamed in the car, and ran into the hospital. I burst into his room, trying to hold back tears. He was sitting up, and when he saw me he smiled and said, "Hello, Sunshine. Everything's going to be okay."

I wanted to believe him. When your father assures you that everything will be okay, how can it not be? He was able to come home shortly after that, and he seemed to get better—the power of positive thinking and hope on all our parts. He and Mom had a quiet, pleasant summer together, and she returned to being extremely attentive. I went off with Carl to a big church camp meeting in Ocean Grove, New Jersey, for two weeks of Bible study. We would attend morning lessons in a large auditorium, and in the afternoon we walked along the beach, treating ourselves to ice cream, or sitting on blankets in the sand talking to the other students who were there.

It was a wonderful, shining time I needed beneath the gathering storm clouds. God was preparing me for the next disaster, the tile in the mosaic of my life that has been created day by day, year by year.

It was August, 1976. George "Sonny" Hlopak, the man I'd never found fault with, the pillar of our family, friend to all he met and the best earthly father a girl could ask for, was dying. He'd been diagnosed with pancreatic cancer that had progressed rapidly, at a time when treatments for this type of cancer were limited and rarely successful. It's the kind of shocking prognosis that takes your breath away and never gives it back. It raged through his entire body. How can you describe — if it were even possible — the sudden and terrifying transformation of a man ravaged by disease? One day he seemed perfectly healthy, the fun-loving, God-fearing man who had been my rock since birth, and the next his body was collapsing in on itself, literally turning him into a shell of the father I'd known. The only grace to it was how quickly it accomplished its mission of taking his life: a mere six weeks would pass between the time he found out this terrible news, and the time that news wouldn't matter anymore. He would be at peace.

CHAPTER EIGHTEEN

Going Home

1976

Those six weeks felt as if I were living life on a roller coaster. One day our hopes would be high, convinced Daddy would recover and everything would be fine, then the next day reality would send me crashing down with the certainty there would be no more highs. At times like this, false hope may be the only hope you have, but it's still hope.

Daddy went in and out of a coma twice when he was in the hospital. We all came and sat beside him, doing what we could to comfort him with love. I was there with my mother; my aunts and my grandmother came, my cousins, everyone from the family. We sat in the room not knowing what to expect. One time he came out of the coma and taught me something I'd never imagined: patients we assume are unaware of their surroundings can hear everything. He told me he'd heard my mother and aunt arguing about something, and it had agitated him. It was another life lesson I've never forgotten. Be careful of what you're saying in the presence of someone in a coma. Be sensitive, and don't say things you wouldn't say in front of them—because they're right there.

The last few hours of Daddy's life were among the hardest as he slipped away all too soon. My mother was falling apart as the rock of our lives and the person she'd most leaned on was motionless in a hospital bed. Days earlier Mother had sent me and my cousin to the funeral home to pick out his casket while he was still alive. Her grief at that moment outweighed any sense she had of what was appropriate to ask a teenager to do. But I was my father's daughter, and I handled it with the grit and assurance of a business woman barely 19 years old.

Unfortunately the funeral director was a business person, too. People in that line of work are as determined to succeed as anyone else, and upselling the bereaved may seem tasteless but it's part of their jobs. He took us downstairs at the funeral home to show us a large display of caskets—some black, some brown, some natural colors in various metal finishes. Some of them had brass handles, others had gold trim. It remains one of the most unique showrooms I've ever seen.

After offering us a wide choice of final resting places for our dearly departed, he asked if we would like a boxspring included. It didn't occur to me to ask why anyone buried would need a boxspring, but if we were paying for it I wanted to try it out. I proceed to sit in the casket to see just how comfortable it would be for someone who would never enjoy its comfort. My cousin and I were at least able to get a laugh of out if—a brief, light moment we would remember the rest of our lives.

After selecting a casket for Daddy that did not include boxsprings, seatbelts or a radio, my cousin and I headed off to a diner for something to eat. By then we were completely drained. We were nearly silent through the meal, worn down from the stress of it all and waiting for the next shoe to drop. Our food had arrived and we were just beginning to eat when I glanced out the window and saw two police cruisers pull up. Their lights were flashing, sirens off, two horses from an apocalypse. I knew instantly they were there to tell us Daddy was no longer on the planet.

The next three days were a blur as people arrived at the house with food and flowers. I didn't know most of them, and I watched in silence as my mother greeted them wearing a black dress and pearls. None of them, including her, asked me how I was doing. In a way, this was all for her and about her — her grief, her loss. I was almost a bystander in my own tragedy. The girl who had become the Clean Up Queen, arranging the funeral and assisting with a wake that felt as if it were in some way for me, too, went and bought the plots Mother insisted I purchase next to her and Daddy. At the tender age of 19 I became the proud owner of a small rectangle of land next to my parents' post-life property. Theirs had a headstone, mine did not. That was expected to come later. Once I'd become a landowner of sorts, with my own stake in the afterlife, I quietly slipped into an abyss.

The viewing at the funeral home lasted for three days, during which I looked at Daddy in the casket I'd bought for him, dressed in his finest suit with a Bible resting next to his hand. A hearse would take him on a long drive to my grandmother's church, leading a procession of cars that stretched as far as the eye could see. It was nearly 20 miles to the cemetery, and all along the route, lining the streets, were police cars with officers saluting as we drove by. Daddy stopped traffic that day.

When we arrived at the cemetery there were at least 50 police cars from different states. Hundreds of people were there. Sonny Hlopak got his well-deserved 21-gun salute as he was laid to rest. My mother, consumed with her own grief, did not reach out for me. We stood watching as they lowered the casket and we prepared to drop flowers onto that beautiful mahogany box holding the body of the man I would cherish all my life. I was having trouble letting go of my flower, as if it were one goodbye too many.

My mother nudged me and said it should be me in that casket instead of Daddy. She may have considered it an offhand remark, but it was a knife in my heart. I was shocked by what she'd said, yet I had been so numbed by his illness and death, and the demands that had been made on me so Mother could immerse herself in her own pain, that I felt almost nothing. How can you hurt someone who was already so numb that I had to bite the inside of my mouth to make tears fill my eyes? I knew if I started crying I would never stop.

The house that night was painfully quiet. It was just Mother and me, alone after the hustle and turmoil of the last six weeks. I believed I knew how it felt to have the nails pounded into my own coffin. I went downstairs to where Daddy kept his tools. They were all exactly where he'd left them, arranged just-so for his projects. The saw, the hammer, the wrenches, all hanging perfectly still. There was even paint that had never been cleaned up after his working on one thing or another. I was screaming inside, knowing no one noticed it from the outside. Daddy, I wondered, how could you leave me with her?

CHAPTER NINETEEN

Get Me Out of Here

1977

Sometimes life throws you a curveball you never saw coming. You hadn't wound up for the pitcher or swung the bat, but that ball hits you right in the stomach. That's how felt it after Daddy went home to be with his heavenly father. My life seemed to be a nightmare I couldn't wake up from. One minute I'd been loved and adored by a father who took the greatest care of me and a mother I'd always known loved me, and the next I was at the whim of that same mother's out-of-control mood swings. Everything became quiet in the house as the flood of people coming and going quickly gave way to stillness. They'd given Mother all that attention because my dad Sonny had died. It was almost silent now —just the two of us, with no noise or parade of strangers offering their condolences. There was no laughter, no Sunday music playing on the stereo, no one showing up at the door. They'd all disappeared and left us to figure out life without him on our own. How could I make sense of these things when I was barely 19 years old? My mother had lost her anchor and her husband. How could I return to the stream of life, let alone swim against a current that had washed everything away? I realized at that young age my mother's demons were not mine to struggle against, they were hers and they'd all been let loose since the funeral. She was attacking me almost daily. I couldn't breathe in that house. I'd hated it since my father had to buy it on short notice to avoid paying capital gains when we came back from California. Now it felt like a tomb. I didn't know which end was up.

"Good afternoon," Mother said one day. "Let's go out for lunch."

We went to a sandwich shop, and after barely eating while we stared at each other, no words of comfort being offered by her, the server brought a check. Mother told the her she wanted two checks. When the server returned, Mother handed me mine for $1.78 and said, "Daddy's gone, you're on your own now."

What seemed like yet another cruel moment became the catalyst for my escape. I'd heard through a church friend of a place called His Hill Bible School in the small town of Comfort, Texas. I had no idea what I was about to get into, but it was to the west and far away from my mother and all that pain our move back to New Jersey had created. So it was to the west I fled. I arrived at the San Antonio airport packed with just one small bag that I had thrown together over the last week, supported by my very small bank account. The only real possession I took was my bicycle. I was going off to Bible school, yet I'd been in such a rush I'd forgotten to bring my Bible. I had no idea at the time that the lessons I was about to learn would stay with me for the rest of my life. I'd never done anything like that before. I'd never left home without family or friends, but there I was, getting off an airplane, dragging my bicycle through the terminal, trying to identify a stranger sent to pick me up to take me to the school. I knew almost nothing about it except that it was both a way out and a way forward.

I was met by a very nice lady who held up a sign with my name on it. All the way back as she drove us in the dark she talked and talked, too much really when all I wanted in those moments was silence — in the car and in my heart. I needed to find peace in my soul, and I hoped as fervently as I could that this was the way to it.

We went up this long road to the top of a hill. The stars were out, and the brightest star I'd ever seen welcomed me to His Hill Bible School. The name was on a large sign with a small chapel to its right. Minutes later I was led into a dormitory with four other girls. It would be the first time I'd ever had to share a bathroom with strangers. As unsettling as the experience was, it was about to help me heal little by little, something I'd been afraid to hope for when I got off that plane.

His Hill Bible School is an extension of the mission laid out for an organization called Torchbearers that now reaches across the country and globe. Begun in England in the devastating aftermath of WWII, Torchbearers was the vision of Major W. Ian Thomas, who joined with his wife Joan to found a refuge for Europe's young people, many of them shocked from years of war. The Thomases initially provided them with lodging and food in a holiday setting, while also giving them instruction from the Bible.

The German youth who arrived in those early days began calling themselves themselves the "Fackeltraeger" or "carriers of the torch," and from that they came to be known as "Torchbearers." Today the ministry enjoys a presence on every continent, with 25 different centers offering change and hope to thousands of people every year.

Comfort, Texas, is a one-horse town just 47 miles from San Antonio. The name seems appropriate as the home of an institution offering spiritual comfort to so many people, including me as a 19-year-old in great need of it. The land the School sits on was donated by an amazing woman named Johnnie Estelle Merchant, whose deep Christian faith compelled her to help the School establish a permanent home. She understood the importance of creating a sanctuary where young hearts could build relationships rooted in faith. Recognizing the need for a dedicated space for spiritual education and fellowship, she generously donated 84 acres of land to serve as the foundation for His Hill Bible School. She also chose to live there for the rest of her life, and died peacefully on the property in 2006.

Since I first arrived all those years ago, the school has played an important role in shaping pastors, leaders, and laypersons who've contributed to churches and ministries around the world. My own life bears witness to its influence, and my experiences there shaped the person I became in ways that have never changed, offering me a center to my own being and shelter in life's many storms.

CHAPTER TWENTY

Texas Skies

1977

Texas. The name itself sounds strong, conjuring images of wide-open spaces and flat, hot land. Words like these are often used to describe the state, but those wide-open spaces are also beautiful, with a million stars shining in the night sky, and a stillness to that vast, hot land. There's no place else like it, and when you spend real time there it gets into your soul. It becomes part of you, and part of the memories you'll always cherish.

When I drove through Texas with Mother and Father we never saw hills, just cattle grazing, oil wells, and flat land that seemed to stretch to infinity. I never imagined there were such beautiful hills as the kind I found in the Hill Country of Texas, with its cypress trees and cool breezes blowing by the Guadalupe River. And in the small town of Comfort, you'll find a place to roam and search your soul.

I was a mixed-up kid depositing myself smack in the prettiest part of Texas. Bluebells, green grass—who would have thought I'd find a place there to heal and grow? Not into a religion, but into a real relationship with my heavenly Father. It all happened there, and it came with a trade: I'd have to work for my peace, and pay for my healing with commitment and duty.

Life at His Hill was very structured. We had Bible instruction in the morning, followed by afternoon and evening classes except on Wednesday. That was the day everyone worked. The boys would go off to cut down trees for new buildings and other labors that required strength, while the girls worked in the office sending out mailings, or cleaning cabins and cooking. One of the directors had the idea we could grow corn, which didn't work out well.

I didn't like the idea of being self-sufficient when it involved working like that, so one day I complained. I wanted to see the fruits of my labor, not just in sending out mailing or cleaning and cooking. The following Wednesday I was led to the empty cement inground pool and given a half dozen gallons of paint and some brushes. My job was to paint until it was complete. There I was painting this big, concrete hole in the ground on a hot Texas day. I have to thank a gentleman named Wayne who came to check on me from time to time, bringing me water and making sure I hadn't passed out in the heat.

I did my job, painting and painting, and before long I found myself screaming out to God so loudly I thought everyone on the hill would hear me. I cried and yelled. I let out every emotion I had, releasing all the pain of losing my dad Sonny to cancer. My mother had put me through so much, and how in the world had I ended up in Bible school? I'd always been a good kid but I wasn't a great student, especially not of the Bible, but that day was a turning point.

I met Jesus more personally than I ever had in my life. I surrendered everything to Him—every hurt, every disappointment and need. When Wayne came to check on me at the end of the day he found me exhausted but changed. He taught me a life lesson I've never forgotten. "God is in the details," he said. "Every snowflake is different, every leaf, every branch on every tree, they're all unique. Don't forget how different you are, too, but remember God loves you. He made you, and he's giving you a spirit. Don't lose it, Kim, ever." After that day at the pool, everything changed.

I wasn't afraid to walk at night under the stars. There were animals sharing the darkness with me, but I was never concerned. Sometimes I'd see an armadillo crossing the trail. I knew they were nearly blind and deaf, relying on their keen sense of smell to navigate their environment. I also knew some of the immigrant camp workers ate them, and that the animals were prone to the bacteria that causes leprosy. But out there by myself at night, I wasn't worried about any of it.

I knew after that day at the pool that I was never truly alone. I wasn't anxious or frightened when the other kids went home for holiday and I spent the time by myself in the cabin. It was the most unique feeling I'd ever had, this sense of being accompanied by a heavenly Father. I was still a bit of a rebel. Once when I'd snuck back into class after riding a horse, the teacher, who was on to my misbehavior, told me to quote from Hezekiah 7:7, a Bible book that didn't exist. I spent several minutes looking for the chapter and verse before I realized there was no such thing. The other students must have known what I'd been up to as well, considering I smelled like the horses.

I didn't know chapters and verses the way some students did, but I learned more than I ever expected to through all the trials, all the hardships and challenges in my young life. God had never left me, I just hadn't realized it before. To this day I often turn around and hurry back to the saving grace of my Lord and Savior.

There was another time my rebellious spirit got me in trouble. I wanted to sit in that beautiful Texas sun. It was only February but the sun felt good, and us girls were in the kitchen baking bread. It was the same recipe we always used and it was delicious. It had cracked wheat in it, thank goodness, because it worked as a cover for my less-than-stellar judgement. I got the idea we could put all the bread outside in the sun and it would rise faster. We'd be able to enjoy ourselves and sit in the sun while bread rose. They all agreed, since I was a great salesperson even then. I could sell snow to an Eskimo. So we sat around having a wonderful time while the bread took care of itself—all 25 loaves.

I looked at all that bread after we'd had our fun and discovered that a trail of sugar ants had found it first. They had swarmed all over the loaves. I knew we had two choices: either throw the bread out and start over, or bake it with the ants inside. We baked it and the girls avoided eating bread that entire week.

Through it all I learned that Jesus does not spare any of us from the pains of living in a fallen world. But it means we're never facing these things alone. Because of Original Sin, we've been separated from our Creator and nothing we do on our own can get us right with God. We're physically and emotionally unable to do this. It's only by surrendering and accepting the gift of His free love and salvation that this can be found. Jesus died on the cross, He did all the work. We just need to ask Him to enter our hearts and spirits. I learned I will still mess up, but I will always be loved by my true Heavenly Father.

There we so many joys there in the hills at the Bible School. I made friends I've never forgotten, some of whom remain part of my life to this day. Everything turned out exactly as it was supposed to for this young girl with her bicycle, heading off to the Texas Hill country without the Bible I'd forgotten.

CHAPTER TWENTY-ONE

Truth Be Found

1979-2015

The mosaic pieces of my life were coming together. It's been many years since I left the Hill Country of Texas and that small town so appropriately called Comfort. So many grown-up things have happened. I got married. I had children of my own. I forged a career in real estate. I know it's all a natural progression, one that each of us goes through as life forges ahead. I learned how to navigate this journey from my dad Sonny. I've been very contented with the ups and downs of my adulthood, and I know whatever steadfastness I've had came from Daddy.

My mother married Gene after Daddy passed away. Gene had given his first wife Helen $1 million and the house in California. Then he had come running after Mother. It only seems fitting that the two best friends—Gene and Sonny—would share the same woman. Mother remained married to Gene for almost 10 years before he passed away. He was laid to rest next to Daddy, his longtime best friend and business partner, in the very cemetery where years earlier I had watched Daddy's coffin lowered into the ground. The two of them were together, whether in business or sharing the same woman, or their bodies lying next to each other in a cemetery plot.

It wasn't long after Gene died that I received a phone call from Mother saying she needed me to meet her as she undertook a reunion with Gene's first wife Helen. It was summer, and I was away with my husband and children. Still being the dutiful daughter I'd always been, I drove back up as requested. Knowing Mother was meeting her long-ago best friend, I informed my husband that this could be a very dramatic moment, and to please excuse me if I needed to stop a cat fight I believed could occur between the two women. As we approached the house of a mutual friend of both women, I noticed a very frail, almost skeleton-like woman. Her hands looked bony, and her hair was white. Mother stood next to her. The two of them connected eye-to-eye. Helen came up and playfully tweaked my mother's nose, and I realized this would not be a moment of anger. Helen and my mother who stole her husband locked arms, hugged and kissed. I've never seen a sight like that before or since. The love between these two women was so strong, beginning when they were young, and fortified by the friendship between their husbands. The men had been business partners, and Gene had left Helen for the woman she was now embracing, my mother. It rocked me to my core.

They spent time together, walking arm in arm, laughing and enjoying each other's company. The memories of youth between them had not diminished. They spent the rest of the summer together. My mother was there the day Helen died.

She held her friend as she passed from this life. Mother claimed Helen's body after death and had her cremated. The ashes are sprinkled now where Daddy and Gene are buried. Helen was laid between them. There's still one plot left for Mother, and it's where she'll have her final resting place.

Their friendship went full circle. The four best friends will rest peacefully together. I still shake my head over the scene I'd witnessed. It showed a kind of love we rarely see, unsure it even exists until we see it.

Mother was someone who seemed incapable of being alone for an extended time. It wasn't long before she began keeping company more and more with old family friends Ted and Carol. It seemed natural. She had been good friends with them for years. She'd helped take care of their children. In a way, it felt like closing a circle.

Ted and his family had been part of my parents' lives before I was born, going back to when Sunny and Loretta moved into their first home together on Shirley Street in Plainfield. Just as Mother was close to Ted and his wife Carol and their children, I was especially close to their daughter, Linda, all my life.

Linda became a constant presence in my world, watching me grow up, teaching me so much over the years. After my father passed away, Linda was the one steady person who never let me down. She never lied to me. If she said she would do something, she did it. She was as direct and steady as my father had been.

Linda, too, had been there before I was born, often staying with my mother and father from the time she was young. Because her own mother was having babies every two years, Linda grew especially close to my mother. Loretta loved Linda like her own child. In many ways, it was as if Linda had been a "practice baby," cared for before I came along.

Linda was nine years older than me, and when we grew and built lives of our own, Linda moved away. I went on to marry and have my own family, and I didn't see her as often as I wished. She eventually moved to Maryland, and surprised me one day with a phone call. She said needed to talk to me, face to face. We arranged a date and time, and when I arrived at her home, she looked so different. I learned she'd been very sick, and that she had cancer. I knew her time on earth was limited.

She still held her strong faith. She told me that if God wanted to heal her, He could, but but if not, she knew she would see me again one day in heaven. She spoke of it as a perfect place filled with peace and happiness, with no sickness or sorrow. She reminded me of what the Bible tells us, that we will be together again. She quoted Revelation 21:4, saying God will wipe every tear from our eyes.

Then Linda told me one more story.

She said, "What I'm about to tell you is unbelievable, but I need you to hear it."

She told me that one day, when she was playing with me and I was about four years old, I became tired. Mother put me in my bed for a nap. Linda didn't want to go back to her own house, so she laid down on my mother's couch in the living room and fell asleep.

She was suddenly awakened by yelling.

She recognized her father's voice, but he wasn't the one whose voice was raised. The people shouting were my father and my mother. Linda said she rolled under the couch so she wouldn't be seen. What she heard shocked her. She said she couldn't believe that my father, the gentleman everyone knew, was threatening Ted, telling him that if he ever caught him around Loretta again, he would kill him.

Linda said it terrified her. She never spoke of it to anyone. Shortly after that day, my parents moved to a different part of town, away from their friends on Shirley Street, and away from Linda, who was still too young to drive and visit us on her own.

The memory haunted her for years. Now, as she sat across from me, Linda was finally confiding in me. She said what she believed she had overheard left a deep dent in her heart. What she remembered, and what she was now telling me, was that she believed I might be her half-sister, and that Ted might be my biological father.

I left Linda's home with a broken heart. I was losing Linda to death, and if what she suspected was true, I was losing my father Sunny all over again.

The weight of it all was almost too much to bear. In some ways, it made sense. I had always felt deeply connected to Ted's children. Still, the thought was overwhelming.

Looking back now, I believe I suppressed that memory. As I grew older, I learned that burying memories often happens when an experience is too emotional, overwhelming, or traumatic. The mind pushes the memory out of conscious awareness as a way to cope with it. The memory isn't erased, it's locked away because remembering it once felt unsafe or unbearable.

Suppressing memories allows a person to survive, to function, and to move forward. And that's exactly what I did, for almost eighteen years. I moved forward in silence, never speaking of what Linda had confided in me: that she believed Ted was my biological father.

Linda passed away shortly after our meeting. I buried that conversation deep in my heart, where it lay dormant all those years, like a volcano waiting to erupt.

Life has its own rhythm. Some people move through life slowly and steadily, like a soft waltz. In my case, life has felt more like jazz, fast-paced, unpredictable, intense. My life has always moved to a quicker beat than most.

Deep down, I needed to know the truth about who I was. It wouldn't change who I am. It wouldn't change how much I loved Sunny Hlopak as my father. But now, I needed to know if the man my mother was spending time with was my biological father.

Ted's wife had passed away several years earlier, and his daughters had asked my mother to take him in and help care for him. I needed to know if this man I sometimes sat with, sharing tea and conversation, was actually my father.

Convinced it must be true, I decided one cold afternoon to finally uncover the truth about who I was. Ted was visiting my mother at our house and sitting on the couch. I had purchased a DNA test and had kept it waiting for the right moment. Ted had been with Mother for quite a long time by then and he'd grown very trusting of me, laughing and sharing moments together. He was sitting in the living room. I went to him and said the kids were conducting a science experiment and needed to see what the swab I had tasted like. I rubbed the inside of his cheek with it and got three samples before mother came rushing down the stairs with a look of absolute horror. She must has seen me from the top of the stairs, or heard what I'd said to him. It was that horribly familiar look she'd given me when I was younger that said she just might kill me this time. Using a second DNA swab, I maneuvered swiftly and managed to slip it into her mouth. I thought I might as well be 100% certain who I really was, on a genetic level at least.

The ghosts of the past were haunting me. I wanted to know the truth of my own beginnings. This was the only way I knew how to be certain. I sent the swabs off to the laboratory and proceeded to wait several weeks for the results. In the meantime, knowing what I'd done and its inevitable results, Mother wrote me a note. It was on my dresser, waiting like an explosive for me to pick it up and read it, not knowing what would be left of me when I did. In the note she told me to go into her room and see a piece of paper that looked like scrap. Was this a mystery of some sort, I wondered? A series of clues for me to follow?

I went to her room and found the paper. The explosive went off: on it was a name I'd never seen in my life. She wrote that this was who my birth father really was. I wondered if she'd gone crazy at last, and if this was another lie. I had to wait until the DNA test came back for Ted. I couldn't possibly have two biological fathers, and the knowledge that my beloved Sonny Hlopak was not one of them had already created a deep, lingering pain.

How could Linda have thought we shared a father? How could I look so much like Ted's daughters? I felt an emotional attachment to Linda, but the note Mother had given me told a very different story. Which one was true? I would have to wait for the mailman to bring me the test results and settle the matter one way or another.

CHAPTER TWENTY-TWO

Secrets Revealed

2015-2025

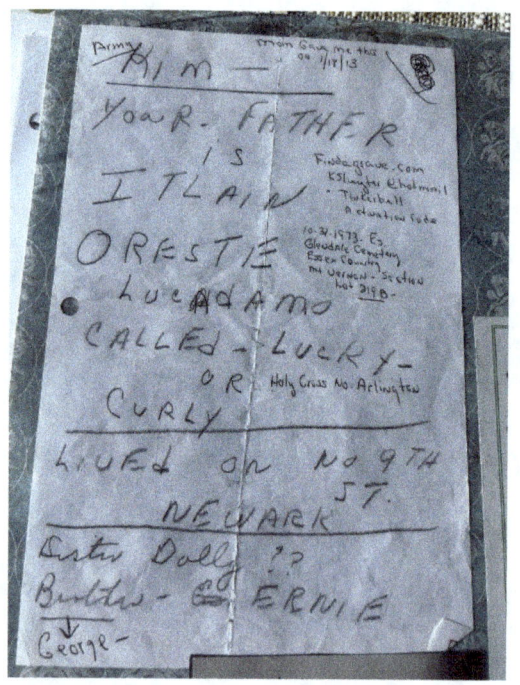

I kept everything to myself. I was too afraid, and too numb, to share this new experience my mother had placed in my hands. I didn't tell my husband. Not my children. Not even my closest friend knew what I was doing, armed with almost no information and no clear direction.

I felt like I was stepping blindly into someone else's story. And yet, this could be my story—and I couldn't ignore it.

I needed the truth. I needed to understand, once and for all, how I came to this planet, by what means, and whose DNA I carried.

It was 4:30 a.m. when I sat on the edge of my bed again, holding that tiny scrap of green paper. It felt like a message from another world. A name I had never heard before stared back at me.

ORESTE LUCADAMO.

Had my mother invented him? Or was this man truly my biological father?

Over the years, my mother had dropped small comments, little fragments that never quite landed. She once said his nickname was "Lucky" or "Curly." At the time, I didn't think much of it. Now my heart ached as I stared at that name, wondering what truth lay hidden in the fibers of that paper, unsure where to begin.

So I turned to the internet.

I set up an account on Ancestry.com and typed in the name of a stranger who might hold the key to my past. I posted a simple inquiry — his name and the few details I had. To my surprise, it took less than twenty-four hours to receive a response.

The person who answered was curious — and cautious. Of course they were. We didn't know each other. How do you build trust over the internet when the truth could be life-shattering?

Then I remembered a small black-and-white photograph of my mother.

She looked to be about sixteen, playing with a toddler. It was clearly winter — everyone bundled up — but their faces were unmistakable. I scanned the photo and sent it to this internet stranger, hoping it might spark recognition.

Within a day, messages arrived.

Each one carried details I never imagined I'd learn. The internet stranger told me the child in the photograph standing beside my mother was *his* mother as a young girl. He was working on his family genealogy and believed he could help me.

Every piece of information pulled me deeper into a history I never knew I was connected to.

By day, I met my day-to-day responsibilities, quietly hiding this secret. By night, I returned to the internet, chasing fragments of who I might be. Names. Dates. Relationships. Each message helped sketch the outline of a life that had always been tied to mine, even though I didn't know it.

I was so consumed with investigating that I didn't pause long enough to notice the emotional shift happening inside me.

What would this new information do? Would it open doors to experiences I had lived but had been told never happened? Would it confirm feelings I had buried?

I didn't know where this journey would end. I only knew I had to find the truth.

And slowly, quietly, it began placing a large mosaic piece into the center of my life.

CHAPTER TWENTY-THREE

Italian Way of Life

2015

One day, I began to feel like a spy in my own home, living my normal life by day, then returning to the hidden search by night. I kept it from everyone. The information from my internet stranger continued to pour in. Names. Photographs. Stories about people I never knew existed, all connected to the man my mother had always called *Lucky*.

Then the DNA results arrived.

I let the envelope sit unopened for days, afraid of what it might confirm. When I finally gathered the courage to open it, the first page confirmed what I had long assumed.

Loretta Naguszewski Hlopak Patz is my natural mother.

The second page confirmed that Ted was not my biological father.

My mother's note had been telling the truth after all.

When I tried asking her questions, she grew angry whenever I pressed. Still, the more I learned, the more certain I became that the truth would change everything I believed about my heritage. I had grown up thinking I was half Polish and that my father, Sonny, was English with a little Hungarian mixed in. Now it seemed there was a part of me I had never understood.

A part that suddenly explained so much.

My lifelong attraction to Italian cuisine, from the food and music, to even the boys I had been drawn to when I was younger, now felt like more than coincidence. I remembered getting in trouble at my private school for using my hands too much when I talked. My teacher made me sit on my hands so I wouldn't use them telling a story. I didn't know it then, but using your hands to emphasize emotion is such an Italian trait.

I guess I had been Italian all along and never knew it.

Then one day, my internet stranger called me.

He was completely convinced that I was his relative. In fact, he believed I was his first cousin. Now I had a name to go with the voice: Steven. He came into my life for only a brief moment, but with such generosity and depth that he never realized how much he changed everything I thought I knew about myself.

How do you grow up believing you are one person, living one story, only to discover there is an entire chapter you never knew existed? And how do you prepare for the emotional weight of that truth?

I needed to know more.

Steven sent pages and pages of information. Photographs spilled out of my printer, one after another. Then one day, he sent me a picture of my biological grandmother.

I almost fell over.

It was as though I was looking at my youngest daughter. The resemblance was undeniable.

Soon after, Steven sent another email — another gift.

Dear Kim,

I was born about a decade after Oreste died, so I never met your natural father. However, he has one surviving sibling — his youngest sister, Alberta. She would have much more information. I'll call her today or tomorrow and try to arrange a phone conversation between the two of you.

I'm also sending you a photo of your natural father's gravesite in Glendale Cemetery in Bloomfield, New Jersey. He's buried alongside his parents and two siblings. I also have documents about the family history and immigration to the U.S. that I can email you soon.

There's just one detail I need before I call Alberta. Oreste dated your mother during World War II while he was in the Army. Do you know if you were born around that time or later? I want to get the timeline right before I explain everything to her.

Within minutes, I was writing back.

From what my eighty-four-year-old mother had told me, she had known the Lucadamo family since she was fourteen, when she moved from the farm in Pennsylvania to Newark, New Jersey. She said she babysat for them and spent time at their apartment on Springfield Avenue. Later, the family bought their first house somewhere on Ninth Street in Newark, but she continued to stay in touch with Oreste.

When he was in the Army, he carried a small photograph of her, one they took together at Olympic Park when he showed her the sights. He even had a painting done of her in Paris.

I still have that painting.

With all this new information, Steven arranged a phone call between me and my natural aunt. She was living in Florida and in her nineties. We scheduled the call for that afternoon.

I drove to my mother's house. I wanted Loretta to be part of this from the very beginning.

When I dialed the number, a sweet, strong voice answered. My natural aunt. Someone whose blood ran through me. She welcomed me with warmth, as if she had known me my whole life.

She told me my mother had promised to bring me to the family after my father George passed away—but she never did. My aunt said she had waited and wondered what had become of me. She shared what she could about her brother, always calling him by his nickname, *Lucky*.

It seemed the family had always known about me.

Somewhere deep inside, I felt I had met some of them before—faint childhood memories stirring just from the sound of her voice. It was as though a missing connection in my heart had finally been filled.

Now I had an aunt. A real aunt. Aunt Bert.

Within weeks, I flew to Florida. I needed to touch her, to see her with my own eyes. I was blessed to meet her two beautiful daughters, Cynthia and Winifred. Though they were much older than I was, they welcomed me without hesitation. Given that my biological father was 19 years older than my mother, it made sense that there would be such a large age gap between me and my cousins, and that Aunt Bert would be in her nineties. What a gift it was that God had kept Aunt Bert alive to be the golden thread tying my life together.

We sat in a café for nearly four hours. I brought my oldest daughter with me. I needed someone else to hear these stories—because with this incredible blessing, some of the hardest moments of my childhood finally began to make sense.

CHAPTER TWENTY-FOUR

Mosaic Pieces Fall Into Place

2015

There's a cool breeze in the evening as I watch an American flag flutter from its pole. I'm resting on a bench outside the nursing home where my mother has lived for the past two years. She is 97 now, and this place has become her home. I brought her here just two years ago. She lives only ten minutes from my house, and her grandchildren and great-grandchildren visit often. Her mind is still sharp. She knows us.

Her body, however, has reached a stage where she can no longer stand.

Loretta is well liked here. The staff and residents all notice the spark in her eyes — the same spark she carried all those years ago. The hardest part of this transition was getting her here. She had suffered several strokes while living alone. Her companion, Ted, had passed away ten years earlier. She had a small dog for company and neighbors who checked on her regularly. We did everything we could to keep her in her own home, but eventually age took its toll.

I laugh when I think about her weighing only ninety-eight pounds. She could eat baked goods all day and still keep that remarkable figure. She's famous here for flirting with the men in the cafeteria, an irrepressible part of who she is. Some things never change.

What *has* changed over the past decade is everything I learned after my mother left me a note on her dresser, one meant for me to find. That note began my journey to discovering who I truly am.

I learned first about my natural father. He was one of eleven children—three girls and eight boys. My natural grandmother, Gilda Julia Arciero Lucadamo, was married in 1899 at the age of nineteen in Brooklyn, New York. She had been born in 1880 in Sparanise, Caserta, Italy, and arrived in the United States through Ellis Island when she was only fourteen years old. She was nineteen years younger than her husband and gave birth to eleven children.

They lived in an apartment building on Springfield Avenue, the same building my mother's mother, Sarah, and her husband Alex moved into after leaving their farm in Pennsylvania. It was Sarah who sat with Gilda on the rooftop of that building and read her fortune, telling her that her son "Lucky" would return from the war. He did—otherwise, I would not exist.

It was there that my mother, Loretta, met Oreste. He was nineteen years older than she was, standing 6' 2" tall, with a solid 180 pounds and curly blond hair. He took her to Olympic Park, where a photograph was taken—one he carried with him into World War II. It was in that home that my mother learned to make the best Italian spaghetti sauce, despite being a terrible cook. She learned it from my true grandmother, with the help of cousins I would one day discover—two through the internet, and two I met in Florida after several trips.

Without them, my mind would still be wandering, longing for truth. They helped me piece together memories I never understood, like the time I fell while skating as a child, and a man picked me up. He didn't smell like my father. That man was my natural father, Lucky.

He bought me a blue snowsuit when I was five. I remember visiting a beautiful lake house, people petting my hair, teasing me warmly, and giving me a doll. I remember being sad on the car ride home, because my mother threw that doll out the window so I wouldn't tell my father Sonny that I had met new people.

Lucky saw me several times throughout my childhood. He paid Ellis in California to watch over me. He was the voice on the phone telling me I had nothing to be afraid of, and telling my mother she would know how to reach him if she ever needed him.

Everything began to make sense. Why my mother sometimes called me a liar. Why she guarded her secret so fiercely. I can see now how her treatment of me reflected the weight she carried.

When I turned sixteen, Lucky died. That was when my mother began to beat me. I believe her loneliness became unbearable. Perhaps Lucky was the love of her life, and not my father. Sonny was a good man. To his dying day, I don't believe he ever knew I was not his biological child.

My mother told me she never told her sisters. Not even her mother, Sarah. And it all made sense when I turned thirteen and my hair began to curl. I remember my grandmother asking, "Did you give Kim a permanent?" I remember my mother rushing me into the bathroom with a straightening iron.

The fear she carried must have been agonizing—to love me, yet struggle with what I represented. A love she could never truly have. A secret that could destroy everything.

George and my mother had been married nine years before I was born. The family assumption is that he could not physically have children, and that she and Lucky carried on their affair long enough to give her the child she always wanted.

Through my cousins, I learned that my natural father was a wonderful cook, a gift passed down to my daughters. I learned that he loved life, laughed easily, smiled often, and had sparkling blue eyes. They say I carry those same qualities. I've seen photographs of him. The resemblance is undeniable — my son looks just like him.

There are news articles that suggest a more complicated story, but that's a secret I will never pursue.

What matters is this: somehow, he always watched over us.

The greatest gift from all of this discovery is that the holes in my heart and mind have healed. Especially through one cousin I adore — fourteen years older than me, full of life, sharing the same faith and love of God. I am truly blessed.

God placed the mosaic pieces together.

I understand now why George passed away early. The truth might have broken his heart beyond repair. I am grateful he never knew.

I am grateful, too, that my mother no longer carries her secret alone. In a strange way, it has unburdened us both. Over the past two and a half years, a deeper bond has formed between us.

Despite the times I tried to walk away from God, He never let go of me. He always pulled me back. Looking back now, I can see it clearly — something stronger was always ahead of me, pulling me through the darkest seasons.

The final mosaic piece has been placed.

Forgiveness.

CHAPTER TWENTY-FIVE

I Am My Mother's Child

2025

I am my mother's child.

Writing this book has cultivated a deep self-awareness in me through the telling of these stories. Many personal questions were asked and answered, and I hope that somewhere in these pages, it might help you on your own journey toward finding your true self.

I am my mother's child.

I am also the child of an affair — something that may sound uncomfortable or even shocking to some people. But the truth is this: no matter how you arrive on this planet, God has a plan for you.

It took me decades of unraveling — through hurt, betrayal, confusion, mystery, and forgiveness — to understand that truth. For many years, I was angry with God for taking my earthly father, Sunny, home far too soon, when I was still just a child. But looking back now, I see something I couldn't see then. God's timing isn't ours. Everything in my life was revealed only when I was mature enough to handle it.

I'm not an accident. Nor are you.

There is a purpose in our being here, and I still have to remind myself of that. Every life has a story. What matters is what we do with the life God has given us.

As I reflect on my life, I remember that while my mother loved me, she lived a very difficult life — one that spilled into mine in ways I didn't always understand as a child. She taught me many things: some wonderful, some necessary, and some painful.

One of the hardest lessons she taught me was not to trust people blindly, that what people say does not always match what they do. I learned early that actions speak louder than words. People can say what they think you want to hear, to manipulate you or to make themselves feel better, but in the end, it's their actions that leave the deepest mark.

She taught me to be grateful for what I have. She taught me not to let the sun go down on an argument — you never know if you'll see that person again to make things right. She taught me that life does not get easier — you just get stronger. She taught me that you will lose friends when you start taking your life more seriously.

She taught me that people come into your life for a reason, a season, or a lifetime, and you should cherish the memories. And one of the greatest lessons: forgiveness is often required to move forward.

Moving forward can feel like dragging yourself through thick mud — sticky, heavy, pulling you backward. But somehow, when you finally reach the other side, no matter how long it takes or what it costs, you find yourself renewed.

It took me a long time to reach the place where I could finally say:

I am my mother's daughter, and I'm proud of it.

I had to forgive my mother for the hurt she caused me — some she may have known she was doing, and some she likely didn't. When you grow up in a home that is loving yet confusing, your mind finds places to hide, or it risks being crushed. Without hope, strength, faith, and digging deep into my heart, I would not be the woman I am today.

Every layer, every painful experience, moved me forward, even when it hurt.

My mother taught me that no matter how bad things get, tomorrow is another day. When we wake up with the attitude that we can begin again, life becomes survival — and sometimes, even beautiful.

She taught me the kindness of strangers. I remember thinking it was odd, coming from a woman who could be hurtful toward me at times, yet I watched her hold doors open, smile at people, touch a shoulder just to say hello. Ted, her friend, once said, "*Loretta has a thousand friends, but few of them know her name.*"

I find myself doing the same now — smiling at someone who looks sad, acknowledging a stranger's existence. Sometimes people don't need fixing. They just need to be seen.

I remember going with my mother to see *Pollyanna* when I was a child. It was icy outside, and she fell and cut her knee badly. Still, she insisted on taking me to the movies. She sat there beside me with a kitchen towel wrapped around her bleeding leg, never complaining.

In the movie, Pollyanna played the "glad game" — always finding something to be thankful for. At one point, Pollyanna wanted a doll, but instead received crutches. Her father told her to be glad she didn't need them. The message was simple: be thankful for what you have.

Somehow, even as a child, I knew my mother needed me to see that movie with her. Looking back now, I understand why.

Another memory comes from Woolworth's, the old five-and-dime store. My mother and I would sit at the long counter where you could order anything from eggs to hamburgers to hot fudge sundaes, which we both loved. Above the counter hung strings with balloons tied to them. Inside each balloon was a piece of paper with a number on it—when you popped the balloon, that's what you paid for your ice cream.

While we waited, I wandered down an aisle looking at the merchandise. When I turned back, I saw a live mouse running straight toward my mother. She panicked. I thought it was hysterical. She jumped up on a stool, then onto the counter, while a waitress tried to catch the mouse with a paper cup.

Years later, my mother told me why she was so terrified. As a child, she had been sent down to the cellar on the family farm, where a mouse ran toward her—and that moment triggered something far worse. That was when she told me she had been molested by her uncle. I finally understood how deeply trauma can live inside someone, waiting to be triggered by something small.

My mother showed up again and again for the people she loved. She cared for her sister Irene through pancreatic cancer. She was there when Sunny died. She was there when her second husband, Gene, died. She was there when her friend Ted died. She outlived nearly everyone she loved—and still, she chose kindness.

She lived through war, abuse, loss, and heartbreak—and still, she chose kindness.

She drove a school bus for over fifty years—a five-foot-two, barely one-hundred-pound woman with a perfect driving record. She waited for parents to come outside. She brought extra snacks. She decorated her bus for the seasons. She never left a child alone.

She wrote thank-you notes. Sometimes on paper plates. Sometimes just a smiley face. She showed up.

When I needed help with my children, she never once said no. And while I sometimes felt jealous of the love she gave them, I now see it as the gift it was. I try to be that for my grandchildren now. Sometimes healing skips a generation.

Deep down, I know my mother loved me. And I believe she did the best she could with what she had.

I am trying to break the curses passed down through generations. I am doing the best I can with my own children and grandchildren. My hope is not perfection—but peace, faith, healing, and salvation.

Writing this book, I sought answers. And I found them. I am glad I am my mother's child. But most of all—

I am my Father's child. My Heavenly Father's child. It doesn't make me perfect. It makes me forgiven.

Thank you for reading my book. I hope it stirs memories, questions, and reflection in your own life journey.

With love and gratitude,

Kim Cook